THE FINNISH DILEMMA

The Royal Institute of International Affairs is an unofficial body which promotes the scientific study of international questions and does not express opinions of its own. The opinions expressed in this publication are the responsibility of the author.

The Institute and its Research Committee are grateful for the comments and suggestions made by Professor J. J. Holst, F. B. Singleton, and Anthony Upton who were asked to review the manuscript of this book.

GEORGE MAUDE

The Finnish Dilemma

NEUTRALITY IN
THE SHADOW OF POWER

Published for
THE ROYAL INSTITUTE OF
INTERNATIONAL AFFAIRS
by
OXFORD UNIVERSITY PRESS
LONDON NEW YORK TORONTO
1976

Oxford University Press, Ely House, London W.1
GLASGOW NEW YORK TORONTO MELBOURNE WELLINGTON
CAPE TOWN IBADAN NAIROBI DAR ES SALAAM LUSAKA ADDIS ABABA
KUALA LUMPUR SINGAPORE JAKARTA HONG KONG TOKYO
DELHI BOMBAY CALCUTTA MADRAS KARACHI

ISBN 0 19 21 8319 2

© *Royal Institute of International Affairs 1976*

British Library Cataloguing in Publication Data

Maude, George
    The Finnish dilemma: neutrality in the
    shadow of power.
    Bibl. – Index.
    ISBN 0-19-218319-2
    1. Title 2. Royal Institute of International
    Affairs.
    327.471   DK451.7
    Finland-Neutrality

PRINTED IN GREAT BRITAIN BY
EBENEZER BAYLIS AND SON LIMITED
THE TRINITY PRESS, WORCESTER, AND LONDON

CONTENTS

PREFACE

I WOULD like to thank all those who have had the patience and interest to discuss with me the many aspects of Finnish foreign policy. I am particularly grateful to Hermia Oliver of the Royal Institute of International Affairs, London, who did much work in preparing the manuscript for publication, and to Ian Smart, Deputy Director and Director of Studies of the Institute, both of whom gave valuable advice in the final stages of this work. I am also indebted to Professor Roger Morgan for encouragement during a difficult period in the writing of this book.

For obvious reasons the identity of many of the people with whom I discussed the problems dealt with in the following pages cannot be disclosed. This is especially so, because the work is controversial by its nature. I am nonetheless grateful to all my informants and to the enthusiasts for this subject.

A final point: the contemporary Finnish government referred to throughout the text is the coalition government headed by Prime Minister Kalevi Sorsa, which left office in June 1975. With the departure of this government and with the final session of the European Security Conference held in Helsinki in July 1975, this work ends. It is worth while pointing out, however, that with the formation of the new coalition government under Prime Minister Martti Miettunen in the autumn of 1975 the Communists once more entered the Finnish government.

G.M.

University of Turku
August 1975

1 INTRODUCTION

FINLAND borders the north-west frontier of the Soviet Union. As a country it differs from the Soviet Union not merely in geographical size and paucity of population (4,700,000), but also in its social and political system.

Finland is a parliamentary democracy governed, at the time of writing (spring 1975) by a coalition, in which the main parties are the Social Democrats and the Centre Party (formerly the Agrarian Union). Two smaller liberal-type parties, the Finnish National Party and the Swedish People's Party (Finland has a Swedish-speaking minority of something under 7 per cent of the population),[1] are also in the coalition. Finland is a capitalist country; in certain branches of industry state-capitalism plays an important role.[2] Within this capitalist system the interests of the workers are promoted by the Communist Party, which forms the core of a larger Finnish People's Democratic League (generally known by its initials SKDL), by the Social Democratic Party, and by a unified trade union movement (SAK), the principal chairman of which is a Social Democrat, while his deputy is a Communist. The interests of the country's agricultural producers are promoted by an association inevitably referred to by its initials as MTK, which represents both larger and smaller farmers. In this connection it should be borne in mind that the agricultural sector, which is closely bound up with forestry, is still important enough in Finland to provide employment in varying degrees to up to one-fifth of the labour force. The power of the agricultural interest is reflected in the dominant position the Agrarian Union—now the Centre Party—has had in postwar Finnish politics. The influence of this party upon Finnish foreign policy has been great. Socially Finland appears to be a rather radical country with subsidized political parties and political press and unions for both schoolchildren and conscripted soldiers. There is a great deal of social mobility, while educational standards are formally high and the country's trained and educated youth often receive good and even key positions at an early age—the minister of education in the government that was in office till the late spring of

1975, Ulf Sundqvist, gained ministerial office before he had completed the full term of his military service and spent the summer of 1974 away from the ministry completing his army training.

In spite of these obvious features of a radical society, there is also a deep bedrock of conservatism. One of the most powerful expressions of institutional conservatism is the Lutheran church (the second state church, the Orthodox church, has very few members), the larger of the two state churches, to which the overwhelming majority of the population officially belong. In consequence, even the SKDL has found it fitting to put up candidates in the elections for church councils.[3] A second expression of institutional conservatism may be found in the armed forces, in which the ranking personnel are conscripts, the officers and n.c.o.'s being in part drawn from conscripts and in part being a professional corps, though the officers come from a wider range of social backgrounds than might be the case in many countries. Both church and armed forces have served to communicate a feeling of the distinctiveness of the traditional Finnish way of life.

The Finns have an intense feeling of national identity through which the manifold interests of Finnish society seek expression. Reforms thus take place piecemeal, in a context of bickering and bargaining between the interest groups, and in recent years they have occurred without violence. The currently vexing problem of student representation in Finnish university organs has not, for example, led to outbreaks of student violence, even though the students have boycotted the elections. The last outbreaks of trade union violence occurred in connection with the general strike of 1956.

In political life the most obvious expression of institutional conservatism is the Conservative Party itself, or the National Coalition Party to give it its official title. This party, which held 33 seats (June 1975) in a parliament of 200 members, is an important party by Finnish standards, and forms—in curious juxtaposition to its irreconcilable opponents the SKDL, who hold 37 seats—the major part of the opposition to the present government. Though championing the traditional values of Finnish society, the National Coalition Party is too closely identified in the minds of the majority of the electorate with big business and the interests of the upper professional class for it to be accepted as the truly national party it would dearly like to be. On the other hand the Conservatives' belief in the virtues of a property-owning democracy is one that is far from being scorned by electors who vote for other parties. The strength of the Centre Party lies in the votes of farmers who own their own farms, and the two smaller liberal parties persistently proclaim their faith in free enterprise. Most people own their own homes in Finland and the Social Democratic head of the government's Housing Department, Olavi Lindblom, recently spoke of a scheme whereby tenants in rented accommodation could be assisted to become owners of the property in which they lived.

In all these above-mentioned aspects as well as in many others— for example, in the manner in which the country is developing as a welfare state—Finland resembles the Scandinavian countries. While it lacks the trappings of constitutional monarchy that these countries still preserve, Finland has instead a strong presidency.[4] Though the year 1974 was an exception, the president is normally elected by the people, who first elect an electoral college of 300 members, which then elects the president. Presidential power represents in certain matters a considerable modification of the parliamentary system; particularly is this so in the field of foreign-policy making where the president's role is of great importance and where his power has sometimes been exercised—as in the late 40s—in the face of parliamentary misgivings. From the Finnish side it is the exercise of presidential power that has more than anything else laid the foundations first of the *modus vivendi*, and second of the fruitful relationship that has gradually developed in the postwar world between Finland and the Soviet Union.

Historical outline

Finland was part of the Russian empire from 1809 till 1917, when it became an independent state for the first time in its history, since before 1809 it had been a part of Sweden. After incorporation into the Russian empire, however, Finland had been able to retain its Swedish social and legal-administrative system, while Swedish remained the language of higher education and the Lutheran church continued to be the official faith. Economically the free peasantry flourished (there had never been serfdom in Sweden-Finland) and a merchant-industrialist class, whose enterprise was often directed towards exporting, emerged. These distinctive features of Finnish society were given political expression when, in the latter decades of the nineteenth century, the traditional Diet of Four Estates (nobles, clergy, burghers, and peasants) began to meet regularly.

In the meantime in the rest of the Russian empire, in spite of the emancipation of the serfs in 1861, representative organs characteristic of a free bourgeois society failed to develop, for the country continued to be governed bureaucratically. Nevertheless for most of the century the two distinctive Russian and Finnish societies continued to live in a fair degree of harmony, united by a common dynasty, the Romanovs, whose presence in Finland was felt only remotely. In the light of present-day relations between Finland and Russia, it is hardly surprising that this period of Finnish history has attracted increasing attention from both Finnish and foreign scholars. Indeed, Finnish nationalism, in terms of a movement that sought to raise Finnish, the language of the overwhelming majority of the people, to the status of becoming an official and the principal language of the country, grew up under the protection of the Russian empire and was at one period favoured by the imperial authorities as a bulwark against Swedish—i.e. Western—influence. The Finnish nationalist leader J. V. Snellman well knew how to exploit the goodwill of the Russian authorities in the Finnish interest, notably in securing the Language Rescript of 1863, which put Finnish on a footing of equality with Swedish.

From the final years of the nineteenth century until 1917 the Russian bureaucracy tried to extend its sway over Finland, as part of a more general policy to unify the diverse institutions of the empire. This was viewed by a large section of the Finnish educated élite as 'russification'—a cultural onslaught from an inferior civilization. An important section of the Finnish nationalist movement, the Old Finns, as they were called, or the Compliants, as they are often referred to in English, did not participate in passive resistance to the Russian measures but sought conciliation and concessions to reach a *modus vivendi* with the Russians that would preserve the essential parts of the Finnish way of life and its institutions. By 1909, when their representatives left the Senate, the majority of the Compliants felt they had failed. But the significance of their attempt, misunderstood by many of their contemporaries and by the succeeding generation, still lived on. For one of the senators who resigned in 1909 was J. K. Paasikivi, and it was he who, as prime minister from November 1944 till March 1946 and as president from March 1946 till March 1956, laid the foundations for Finland's positive relationship with the Soviet Union that has become known as the Paasikivi Line and is the official foreign policy of the country (see below, pp. 26–7). The policy of cooperation between Finland and Russia that blossomed gradually after Paasikivi's retirement and death into the even more fruitful policy of peaceful coexistence thus has strong historical roots.

After the outbreak of World War I in 1914, young Finnish patriots unsuccessfully tried to win Swedish consent to provide military training for Finns. They then turned to Germany, for Germany was fighting Russia and a large section of the Finnish educated class was culturally drawn to Germany; by January 1915 the Germans agreed to give military training to Finnish volunteers. The battalion so founded was sent to the eastern front in 1916 and participated in engagements against the Russians. After the outbreak of revolution in Russia in March 1917 and with the abdication of Tsar Nicholas II, the imperial regime in Finland collapsed, and on 20 March the Russian provisional government restored Finnish autonomy. Following the Bolshevik revolution in November 1917 the Finnish parliament announced full independence on 15 November, and on 4 December Finland became an independent republic, which was recognized by the Bolshevik government on 31 December 1917 and by Germany, Sweden, France, Norway, and Denmark in January 1918. In fact recognition by the Western powers soon ran into difficulties, and the French temporarily broke off diplomatic relations. This was because, after an initial period of toying with neutrality,[5] the new Finnish state turned increasingly towards Germany.

The main problem that faced the new state was, however, an internal one. A bloody civil war between Reds and Whites began which only ended in May 1918, when the Finnish Reds suffered defeat and retribution at the hands of White forces (which included the Finnish volunteers trained in Germany) led by General Mannerheim, in the final stages of the war aided by German troops (despite Mannerheim's opposition). The pro-German Finns, accepting that Russia was hemmed in on its western borders by Germany, took the *Realpolitik* line that it was in Finland's interest to ally itself with Germany, which was granted wide commercial privileges in return for military and diplomatic help.

One of the leading supporters of this pro-German policy, and an enthusiastic advocate of turning Finland into a monarchy with a German prince on the throne, was none other than J. K. Paasikivi. This episode in his career has been regarded as somewhat out of tune with his general line of thinking,[6] and apologists for the post-1944 Paasikivi Line are obviously embarrassed by it.[7] But Paasikivi's advocacy of a pro-German line in 1918, though woefully mistaken because of his overestimation of German power at that late stage in World War I, was still in principle consistent with his previous and subsequent thinking about foreign relations. His belief was that Finland could not avoid commitment to one or other of the powers, or power forces (later he had some sympathy for a Nordic Defence Alliance). This commitment could take the form either of an understanding of Russia's security needs or of an adherence to some force that would constitute a bulwark against Russia: either way, Finland must face the problem in power terms.

After the collapse of Germany, Finland signed a peace treaty with Russia at Tartu on 14 October 1920. The chief Finnish negotiator was Paasikivi who, after the failure of hopes of German protection, came round to an understanding of the Soviet Union's security needs. He was in fact prepared to grant wider territorial concessions to the Russians than his government would sanction. He especially bore in mind the defence needs of Leningrad—an attitude that drew upon him the opprobrium of many of his contemporaries and the posthumous commendation of Soviet historians.[8]

The Finns continued to fear the emergence of a revivified Russia that would demand back its old possessions, and Finnish leaders felt that they could not trust the Soviet Union. The suppression by the Bolsheviks in 1921 of the Menshevik Republic of Georgia was bitterly reported in Finland; nearer home the government continued to be in dispute with the Soviet Union about the autonomous rights of the Karelian-speaking population of East Karelia—rights that had been guaranteed by Article X of the Tartu peace treaty. All this was evidence for the Finns of the Soviet attitude to border peoples. To the Finnish leaders the Soviet Union was a state different in kind from other states, for it aimed at dominance by means of internal subversion through the manipulation of native communists—the Finnish Communist Party had been founded in 1918 after the civil war. To many members of the Finnish bourgeoisie that war is still known as the War of Independence or Freedom,[9] because despite the Bolshevik recognition of Finland's independence, in their view had the Reds triumphed, the country would soon have been incorporated in Russia again. This fear of internal subversion by external manipulation remained strong in pre-1939 Finland—the equivalent of the Communist Party was proscribed in 1930. In a sense this joint preoccupation with shutting the Soviet Union out and purifying Finland from within diverted attention from a true realization of foreign political problems.

In 1920 Finland had entered the League of Nations, which seemed to offer some kind of answer to its security problems. The League's ideology, with its basis in liberal Anglo-Saxon philosophy and its principle of equality between states, also had some appeal for the important group of Finnish leaders who took inspiration from the West. The power of the League was not omni-present, but this might be advantageous for a small state, which could anyway in an emergency summon the League to impose sanctions. In fact one of the first disputes settled by the League was that between Finland and Sweden over the Åland islands in the Baltic, which had been part of the imperial Russian Grand Duchy of Finland. The islanders, who were Swedish-speaking, begged the Swedish government to accept them as part of Sweden, but a neutral commission sent by the League accepted Finland's claim of sovereignty over the islands and the League endorsed this in June 1921, when it was laid down that they should be completely demilitarized (reaffirming the 1856 prohibition on militarization). Characteristically, one of the most important démarches of Finnish foreign policy was the proposal to the League in 1929 for financial aid to states that were the victims of aggression.

Another indication of Finland's conviction throughout the 1920s —with the continuing weakness of Germany and, equally important, of Russia—that the country could not remain neutral was the proposals it made for security arrangements with the Baltic states and Poland on the one hand, and with Sweden on the other. These proposals fell through, partly because of internal opposition and partly because of the external problem of harmonizing Finnish policy with the policies of these states.

By the 1930s a greatly strengthened Germany and Russia were becoming increasingly antagonistic to each other. The Finns inevitably viewed with extremely bad grace the admission of the Soviet Union into the League in 1934.[10] In the same period the Anglo-German naval agreement of 1935, which authorized Germany to reconstruct its fleet up to 35 per cent of the strength of the British navy, seemed to indicate a British withdrawal from the Baltic and acquiescence in German naval predominance there. Finnish thinking about this turn of events remained unsure. Some believed that Finland could withdraw into neutrality, its position ultimately safeguarded by the 'oppositional balance' existing between Germany and Russia.

On 5 December 1935 the Finnish prime minister, T. M. Kivimäki, made a statement in which he identified his country with the other Northern neutrals. But as time went on this became more and more a question of entering into a Nordic Defence Alliance, i.e. of reviving in some form regional security ideas mooted in the 1920s. With Norway and Denmark manifestly uninterested, the question was one of the possibility of Swedish-Finnish military cooperation, which the Finns sought to effect through joint militarization of the Åland Islands, for which they had asked the approval of the League Council; by the summer of 1939, however, the project had foundered on the opposition of the Soviet Union and on the subsequent fear of the Swedes that they might be dragged into war with Russia through the islands. As Max Jakobson has pointed out, the very intention to fortify the islands was an indication of the League's loss of power,[11] but in practice Finland had already dismissed the League by declaring on 20 May 1938 that it henceforward reserved to itself the right to decide whether or not to apply military and economic sanctions decreed by the League against an aggressor state.

The Finns' answer to the apparently growing security problem became essentially therefore one of withdrawal. Rudolf Holsti, who had been foreign minister from 17 February 1937 to 12 December 1938, visited both Moscow and Berlin to try to ensure good relations with both potentially aggressive powers, but Finland refused to enter a non-aggression pact with Germany, and when the Soviet Union in its turn tried to negotiate joint security plans, the Finns refused to cede the territory which the Russians wanted in order to improve their ability to defend Leningrad, rejecting also an offer of Soviet military aid.

The Nazi-Soviet Pact of 23 August 1939 replaced the 'oppositional balance' between Germany and Russia by friendship, or rather by a breathing-space that enabled both powers to take up positions for the future conflict between them. Soviet pressure on Finland was renewed in the autumn of 1939, when Russia demanded areas on the Karelian isthmus and ultimately the port of Hanko to the west of Helsinki, or, at least, islands near Hanko. But in spite of the wishes of Paasikivi, and Mannerheim's earlier expressed view that some territorial concessions should be made, the Finnish government refused to authorize the significant concessions needed. On 30 November 1939 the Soviet forces attacked Finland without a declaration of war. The Finns, with no security treaty with any other state, fought what was known as the Winter War alone, unable to call on an ally and unwilling in the latter stages of the war to accept the projected British and French aid for fear of a ruinous prolongation of hostilities.[12] The war ended on 12 March 1940, when a peace treaty signed in Moscow ceded to Russia the Karelian isthmus, the whole of the province of Viipuri, border territory to the north, and a thirty-year lease of the port of Hanko.

This defeat and loss of territory drew to a disastrous close the foreign policy of the first decades of independent Finland. But in spite of that policy's obvious failure, and the emphasis on its failure in present-day Finland, this does not mean that the whole body of aspirations characteristic pre-1939 Finnish policy have been rejected. In the first place the Finns have not abandoned their hopes for the creation of a world security system and in this sense a certain parallelism exists between their approach to the League of Nations and the United Nations. Thus both in 1929 and in 1968 (on Security Council resolution 255 see chapter 3 below) they sponsored measures for the protection of smaller states that had become victims of aggression. In the second place, now as in the pre-1939 years, the Finns still nourish the hope of being able to withdraw from a conflict situation between the powers. It is this aspect of Finnish defence policy that gives the edge to Jaakko Blomberg and Pertti Joenniemi's critique of that policy in one of the most important books published in the last decade in Finland, *Kaksiteräinen miekka* (The Double-edged Sword).

On the other hand the Finns have become all too aware of the difficulty of such a withdrawal. The requirement to come to terms with the needs of the dominant great power in the area is a feature of current Finnish policy that finds confirmation in the events of recent history, too.

On 22 June 1941 the Germans invaded the Soviet Union and on 26 June Finland likewise declared war on the Soviet Union. Finnish towns had already been bombed by Soviet planes, perhaps because the Soviet base at Hanko had in its turn been bombed—in fact by the Germans, though the Soviet authorities might have thought that the planes in question were Finnish. At any rate, politically the Soviet authorities still hesitated and Molotov asked for a definition of the Finnish attitude, i.e. from the Soviet point of view the chances of Finland's remaining neutral were not apparently excluded.[13] But Finland entered the war on the German side.

For some time the Finns had had a transit agreement with the Germans, permitting the movement of German troops through their country from the German Baltic ports to Northern Norway. Relations had grown ever more close between Finland and Germany, particularly as the Finns witnessed the annexation by the Soviet Union in June 1940 of Estonia, Latvia, and Lithuania, and the subsequent harsh administration in those lands by the Soviet authorities. In May 1941 Finns had taken part in important military talks with the Germans at Salzburg, though the Finns entered into no clear commitment even then. A strong current of political opinion in Finland, especially among the Right, was clearly on Germany's side. Thus Paasikivi, as Finnish minister to the Soviet Union in 1940–1, firmly believed that Russia was weaker than Germany and that a German victory in Europe was inevitable; it was therefore in Finland's interest, he thought, to enter into a relationship with Germany either directly or under the auspices of a Nordic Defence Alliance under German protection.[14] The fact that prominent Finns held viewpoints like this made natural, if not exactly inevitable, Finnish participation with Germany in the invasion of Russia in 1941.

Nevertheless Finland regarded this war with the Soviet Union as a separate war, which is in fact known as the Continuation War (i.e. a continuation of the Winter War), but as it turned out the Finns had chosen the losing side. In February 1943 the government and military leadership decided that in view of Germany's worsening military position, an attempt should be made to get out of the war, though it was not until 4 September 1944 that the Finnish high command signed a ceasefire with the Soviet Union and fifteen days later an armistice, whereby the Finns had to place their armed forces on a peacetime footing within two and a half months and turn on their German comrades-in-arms and expel them from Finland. Thus by another twist of *Realpolitik*, the Finns came over to the Russian side.

Ever since the historians Leonard Lundin and Anthony Upton questioned Finnish motivation in entering the war against Russia in company with Germany,[15] this Finnish action has been a matter of growing embarrassment to the academics and decision-makers of postwar Finland. But whether Finland drifted into the war or not—and it may be remarked that Finnish leaders had a strong motivation to get back the territories lost in 1940 and to seek a permanent destruction or at least weakening of the Soviet state so that Finland would be left alone in future—the fact remains that participation in this way signified a recognition by the Finns of the impossibility of totally escaping involvement in great power politics. Thus their policy was in open contrast to the pre-1939 policy of seeking a withdrawal from great power conflicts. In postwar Finnish policy we shall find elements of both policies: of commitment to involvement in great power needs and, on the other hand, an aspiration to withdrawal.

The conditions laid down in the armistice agreement[16] were confirmed by the peace treaty concluded in Paris on 10 February 1947. The principal provisions of this treaty re-established the 1940 boundary but also ceded Petsamo to the Soviet Union and leased Porkkala for fifty years as a Soviet naval base; Hanko was returned to Finland. The Åland islands were to remain demilitarized. To the distaste of the Finnish delegation, specific limitations were imposed on the personnel of the Finnish armed forces and the weapons they could use: Article 13 set an upper limit of 34,000 personnel for the army, 4,500 for the navy, and 3,000 for the air force. Article 17 prohibited atomic weapons, guided missiles, certain types of sea mines and torpedoes, submarines, motor torpedo boats and assault craft. (However, in 1962 the signatories to the treaty agreed to allow Finland to have guided missiles for defence purposes.) These limitations were imposed at the insistence of the Soviet Union, for the other main signatory, Great Britain, refused to take a stand against Soviet demands. The United States, not having declared war on Finland, was not a signatory, and American attempts behind the scenes to help Finland did not concern the military clauses. These facts hardly justify G. F. Kennan's argument that the obligations of the treaty were imposed by the Allies and not by the Soviet Union alone.[17]

Despite the fact that Finland had ceded some 12 per cent of its border territory to the Soviet Union, and despite the reparations it had to pay, the Finns felt a sense of relief after the signing of the treaty. In consequence apprehensions increased when it became known at the end of 1947 that the Soviet Union was determined to conclude a mutual assistance agreement with Finland, especially since the news was closely followed by the communist coup in Czechoslovakia. Indeed, one of the Finnish negotiators, J. O. Söderhjelm, wrote pessimistically to his brother in the spring of 1948 that only the establishment of what he called a communist-Russian administration in Finland would ultimately satisfy the Russians,[18] and his pessimism was intermittently shared by Finland's president, J. K. Paasikivi—the man who above all others was nevertheless responsible for getting a reluctant parliament to accept the new Treaty of Friendship, Cooperation and Mutual Assistance that was signed in Moscow on 6 April 1948 and subsequently renewed in 1955 and 1970.[19] There is no doubt whatsoever that in the late 1940s the majority of Finns would have been happier without such a treaty, although the contrast between the present view of it and the mood of the late 1940s could hardly be greater. Nowadays it is lauded on every possible occasion by Finnish politicians and other spokesmen and is often referred to as 'our security treaty'. In fact it has been the earnest endeavour of Finnish policy-makers to accept the treaty as the keystone of Finland's external relations, and it can be demonstrated that clear benefits have arisen from it, so that it has become an essential part both of the reality and the ritual of Finnish foreign policy. However, its significance is complex. While the treaty will be referred to and discussed throughout this work, it is necessary at this point to note the obligations contracted by Finland in the first two (the military-political) articles. Article 1 of the Treaty of Friendship, Cooperation and Mutual Assistance[20] (hereafter referred to as the 1948 Treaty) runs as follows:

In the eventuality of Finland, or the Soviet Union through Finnish territory, becoming the object of an armed attack by Germany or any state allied with the latter, Finland will, true to its obligations as an independent state, fight to repel the attack. Finland will in such cases use all its available forces for defending its territorial integrity by land, sea, and air, and will do so within the frontiers of Finland in accordance with obligations defined in the present agreement and, if necessary, with the assistance of, or jointly with, the Soviet Union.

In the cases aforementioned the Soviet Union will give Finland the help required, the giving of which will be subject to mutual agreement between the Contracting Parties.

Article 2, which is generally referred to as the consultations paragraph, runs as follows:

The High Contracting Parties shall confer with each other if it is established that the threat of an armed attack as described in Article 1 is present.

In justifying, both to themselves and to the world, their acceptance of these articles of the 1948 Treaty, the Finns employ two broadly contrasting lines of argument. In the first place they believe that in the postwar world security arrangements of an explicit nature between lesser and greater states are the rule rather than the exception. From this point of view most states are bound in some way, so that the actions they may take are often predetermined by prior agreements. Thus when the English historian Anthony Upton argued that Finland had had its freedom of action as an independent state narrowed down in the postwar world as a result of Finnish involvement on the German side against the Soviet Union in 1941–4, it was a natural, and not merely impertinent, retort of his young Finnish interviewer to ask how independent England now was.[21] From the Finnish point of view, as President Kekkonen said in a talk to reserve organizations of the armed services in 1970 (the importance of which has been remarked on by the Finnish specialists Blomberg and Joenniemi) the interconnection of states in various security arrangements can be seen as an aspect of international security. At any rate, if the action of most states is circumscribed in the postwar world by a certain relation of dependence upon other states, Finland appears in this regard to be no different from the majority of other states.

But it is the second line of argumentation justifying the 1948 Treaty that has had more significance for the Finns. And according to this, Finland *is* different from the majority of states in the way in which it has arranged its security. For the 1948 Treaty does not bind Finland into any bloc. The Warsaw Pact did not come into being till 1955 and then Finland stayed out of it. Indeed, by making the first renewal of the treaty late in 1955 the Finns succeeded in freeing themselves from the most obvious aspect of their military relationship with the Soviet Union—the presence of Soviet troops in the country. On the face of it at least an implicit bargain appears to have been made, by which the renewal of the treaty was followed by the withdrawal of Soviet troops from the Porkkala base, situated a mere ten miles from Helsinki, which had been leased to the Soviet Union for fifty years under the 1944 armistice agreement, confirmed in Article 4 of the 1947 peace treaty.

Even the bilateral security relationship that Finland has with the Soviet Union is interpreted in the narrowest of fashions by leading Finnish spokesmen. Not merely is it denied by the Finns that the 1948 Treaty constitutes an alliance, but some would go on to argue that it cannot be construed as being basically a military agreement either. This was the viewpoint of the Parliamentary Constitutional Law Committee in 1948 and it has recently been repeated by Risto Hyvärinen, the former head of the Foreign Office Political Department and present Finnish ambassador to Belgrade, in an article in the Helsinki Swedish daily *Hufvudstadsbladet* of 26 April 1974. Keijo Korhonen, when he too was in the Political Department, referred to the treaty as being rather of the nature of a 'reinsurance treaty' than anything else.[22] All this somewhat startling reasoning, by no means accepted by everyone in Finland, derives not merely from the fact that the treaty has undoubtedly other aspects than military ones but also from an analysis of its first two articles stressing their limited nature.

The significant aspects of Article 1 for Finnish apologists are: that the treaty, which is purely defensive by its nature, is confined to cases of aggression against Finland or aggression through Finnish territory against the Soviet Union—it does not apply to aggression against the Soviet Union from any other quarter; that the action of the Finnish forces themselves is restricted to operations on Finnish territory; that the responsibility for defending Finnish territory is Finland's, and at best the Soviet Union will only be a co-participant in this task; that in so far as Russia does aid Finland, this is to be a matter for mutual agreement and this, by implication, gives the Finns a certain reserve power vis-à-vis the Soviet Union—the power, that is, to attempt to handle the situation themselves without Soviet involvement. Finally, it is argued by these interpreters, that Article 1 is descriptive rather than normative. If Finland were to be invaded by the power (Germany) and its allies named in the treaty, the Finns would of course naturally seek to maintain the sovereignty of their country by fighting to repel the attack. 'We would do it anyway'.[23]

Article 2, the consultations paragraph, brief though it is, is also considered to have great importance in the light both of the contention that the treaty is not an alliance and of the possibilities the Finns require to control the situation in a crisis period. For the Finns this consultations paragraph means that the treaty is not an automatic mechanism leading to joint Soviet-Finnish action when a certain circumstance materializes. Before action is taken, there will be a discussion about its necessity and, as the 1961 'note crisis' showed (see below, pp. 20-4), it may even be possible for the Finns to consult about the necessity of having consultations when they may thus—as apparently happened in 1961—persuade the Soviet Union that the situation is not serious enough to warrant consultations.

In consequence of all these considerations, it is hardly surprising to find Finns arguing that the treaty gives them scope for manœuvre —namely for avoiding its implementation. Implementation would after all mean the acknowledgement of a crisis situation, and the fundamental Finnish aspiration of avoiding such an acknowledgement has come out clearly since 1961 in the constant, almost jubilant, references they make to their skilful handling of the events of that year, when consultations were put off. In their search to avoid involvement in crisis situations, it should be noted that the preamble to the treaty includes the phrase 'Considering Finland's desire to remain outside the conflicting interests of the Great Powers', a phrase that is often quoted by Finnish publicists to justify the doctrine of Finnish neutrality.

If the 1948 Treaty is viewed in historical perspective, it will be seen to be a part of a wider series of Soviet measures to protect the Western approaches to Russia. In 1947 the Soviet Union (and its other wartime allies) had concluded treaties of peace with Bulgaria, Hungary, and Romania, and soon afterwards treaties of friendship, cooperation, and mutual assistance with these states—to ensure, once peace had been signed and the Soviet Control Commission had been withdrawn, that Soviet security interests would not be neglected by these countries. The Prague coup was part of the Soviet design to consolidate its position within its sphere.

Thus the Finnish 1948 Treaty shows Finland to be, in a sense, an East European country. But it is precisely at this point that the Finnish insistence on the limited nature of the treaty comes into its own. For the Finnish treaty differs markedly from the other Soviet-East European treaties, which apply in a general state of hostilities with Germany and do not contain consultations paragraphs. Thus if the Soviet Union is invaded by Germany through, say, Poland, Romania but not Finland is automatically involved in the conflict.

In bearing these differences in mind, founded essentially on geography, the continuing difference between Finnish on the one hand and Romanian, Bulgarian, and Hungarian society on the other should also be borne in mind. For the Finnish treaty was neither preceded nor followed by a communist takeover, though rumours abounded both of right-wing and communist coups and the armed forces were alerted to forestall either eventuality.[24] Finland retained its parliamentary democracy.

The German menace and the Finnish-Soviet crises of 1958 & 1961

In 1955 a Soviet commentator spoke of the start of 'a new phase in

Soviet-Finnish friendship': the good-neighbourly relations now developing were based upon 'the principles of equality, non-interference in each others' internal affairs, and mutual respect for national interests'.[25] The Finns felt the same way, and with the return of Porkkala there developed a mood that the Swedish political scientist Krister Wahlbäck described in terms of a post-Porkkala euphoria.[26] The shadow of an external threat seemed to be lifting. Paradoxically this led in certain respects to a reinforcement of traditional Finnish patriotism. The down-to-earth realism of Väinö Linna's novel about the Continuation War (*The Unknown Soldier*, published in 1954) and Max Jakobson's analysis of the Winter War (*The Diplomacy of the Winter War*, 1961, published in Finnish in 1955) seemed to justify the conclusion that the wars after all had not been in vain—Jakobson said as much: in the Winter War the 'country's independence and the nation's freedom' had been maintained. The Soviet suppression of the Hungarian uprising in 1956, which provoked bitter responses in public opinion in Finland,[27] proved what happened to countries that were a part of the Soviet system. Finland was not.

Finland had, of course, its problems. But these were internal. The conflict between capital and labour resulted in a general strike in 1956, and the internal antagonisms of the country became exacerbated by a further dispute between the Left and the Agrarians on the apportioning of the national product. A political solution to these problems would have been the formation of a government from as wide a range of parties as possible. This was attained in July 1958 by the formation of the coalition government of K. A. Fagerholm, which included all parties except the SKDL and Communists. In this government were supporters of Väinö Tanner, a leading member of the Social Democratic Party, a party that had taken a strongly anti-Soviet line during the Winter and Continuation Wars, a line that Tanner was still regarded by the Soviet government as supporting, and Conservatives—a most unpalatable combination from the Soviet viewpoint. President Urho Kekkonen showed a clear lack of enthusiasm for the government,[28] but the fact remained that in 1957 he had himself asked Tanner to head a government.[29]

The Tannerite Social Democrats (and Tanner was now chairman of the Social Democratic Party) were identified in the Soviet mind with a pro-Western and in particular a pro-German policy,[30] and the Conservatives had in addition been accused by Soviet commentators of nourishing revanchist dreams to get back the lands ceded to the Soviet Union in 1944.[31] Since the Communists were left out of the government, though the SKDL had emerged as the largest party in the previous elections, the Soviet attitude to the new government was inevitably hostile.

The Finnish leadership on the whole showed a surprising inability to appreciate the Soviet concern at the development of West German power, even though in looking at Finland's recent past, the role the country played in Russo-German relations was acknowledged—very clearly by Jakobson in his book about the Winter War. It was not, however, appreciated in Finland that the relaxation in tension in Finnish-Soviet relations in the last few years owed a great deal to the change in Soviet attitudes to the German problem—of which the signing of the Austrian State Treaty in 1955 was an important aspect—and much to the spirit of the Geneva talks too; moreover, the Soviet Union had grown confident in the security of its own nuclear and military power. But by 1957 Russia had begun to fear the re-militarizing of the Federal Republic—and in particular the acquisition of nuclear weapons by the Germans. In addition, the Russians feared the spread of nuclear warheads and bases to Norway and Denmark—Khrushchev himself, in an interview in Helsinki on 13 June 1957, informed the Nordic countries of these Soviet fears. A combination of unpleasant factors was seen by the Soviet Union in the project for Danish participation in a Baltic sea-command with Britain and West Germany,[32] a project which was raised again in the 'note crisis' of 1961 (see p. 20). All these developments seemed to be disturbing the existing *low* Northern Balance, for the limited NATO commitment of Norway and Denmark appeared to be in danger of becoming total. Soviet concern thus showed in terms of a Northern Balance situation, even though such a concept was never to be acknowledged by them, and was never to be, as we shall presently see, the ultimate factor for their power calculations in the North. (The Northern Balance is a descriptive term used to cover the diverse security arrangements that have arisen among the Northern European states, by which Sweden remains neutral, while Finland has a security treaty with the Soviet Union and Norway and Denmark are in NATO. Both Finland and Norway and Denmark have avoided a maximum security arrangement with their respective partners.)

At any rate, according to Khrushchev's own account, the neutral peoples of Sweden and Finland should have been worried about this

threatening extension of NATO power close to their borders.[33]
Towards the end of 1957 and in the spring and summer of 1958 the
Soviet government addressed a series of notes to Finland, pointing
out the growing dangers of war due to NATO activity and the need
to stop nuclear tests, which the Soviet Union itself was going to do
unilaterally after March 1958. The Russians asked for the specific
support of Finland in these and allied causes, but though expressing
agreement in principle, the Finns felt that these were primarily
measures for the great powers and it was not until the joint Finnish-
Soviet communiqué of 3 May 1958 that the Finns came out in
support of a nuclear-free zone in Central Europe that would also run
through the North. It was clear that the Finns did not feel any
urgent threat in the North from NATO or, in particular, from West
German militarism.

With the emergence of the European Economic Community,
Western Europe's economic integration took on new dimensions,
and this was a further *political* fact for the Soviet Union to reckon
with. In the meantime Finland had elected a government that the
Russians suspected of being friendly to Western economic interests.
The Soviet Union, in consequence, recalled its ambassador (the
ambassador of the People's Republic of China was also recalled) and
put obstacles in the way of the fulfilment of its own commercial
agreements with Finland, though the Soviet argument is that the
Finns themselves simply neglected to take up the commercial
credits arranged for them by the Russians at the time of President
Kekkonen's visit to Moscow in May 1958. By November the crisis
in Finnish-Soviet relations—generally known as the 'night-frost
crisis'—had run into the much more important crisis in Soviet-
Western relations centring on Berlin. Some Finns, at least, had by
now had enough. In early December the Agrarians left the government, in January President Kekkonen, whose relations with the
Soviet leaders had continued to be good, visited Leningrad; in
between Fagerholm resigned and a minority Agrarian government
was formed. This pleased the Soviet Union and good relations with
Finland were resumed.

The Soviet attitude obviously infringed on the condition of
Article 6 of the 1948 Treaty by which both states pledged themselves
to 'non-interference in the internal affairs of the other state'.
Kekkonen also found it necessary to harangue the Finnish people on
the mistake of allowing the publication of anti-Soviet articles in the
Finnish press and of war books and memoirs with an anti-Soviet

bias. In this the Finnish political system showed a willingness to adapt itself to Soviet wishes, i.e. to accept the inevitability of Soviet interference and to try to forestall it (just as Paasikivi had done by warning the press not to offend Russia).[34] Thus the 1948 Treaty contained something that was greater than its individual parts. Its main purposes were to safeguard against German aggression and to promote Finnish-Soviet friendship. Apparently these purposes took precedence over, say, the terms of Article 6, and there was a faint suspicion already that they took precedence over the statement in the preamble about Finland's desire to remain 'outside the conflicting interests of the Great Powers'.

Kekkonen was at least prepared to admit that 'the danger of war was much closer than he had imagined': this was either a tribute to the Soviet viewpoint or an admission that the Finns had miscalculated the international situation. But the core of the Soviet attitude, the fear of the extension of NATO power in Northern Europe at a time when West Germany was growing in strength, still did not penetrate the Finnish consciousness with sufficient force. The reason for this was that the Finns simply did not fear the West, and certainly not Germany, the greater part of which was now integrated into the West, i.e. accepted by the West—an eminently desirable situation from the viewpoint of most Finns, who could not share the Soviet fear that West Germany would begin to dominate Western Europe and precipitate a renewal of the aggression of World War II against the Soviet Union—this time with the backing of the military potential of the whole of the West.

On two occasions in 1959 Khrushchev warned of the dangers of the Tannerite group in Finland, naming some of the leading Social Democrats, and stating that this group wanted to draw Finland towards military-political blocs, i.e. of the NATO kind. In 1960, some four months after Gary Powers (pilot of the US spy plane) had been shot down en route to Norway, Khrushchev again warned the Finns about the tension of Bundeswehr influence in Norway and Denmark and the planning of a joint Baltic sea command with West Germany.[35]

Finnish attention, however, was not attuned to Soviet fears. The Finns were now proceeding to enter EFTA,[36] which they did in 1961 through the medium of a special FINEFTA agreement that safeguarded the most-favoured-nation status of Soviet trade with Finland. It became important to the Finns to explain their neutrality to the West, but this obviously had a wider import than the EFTA question. For when President Kekkonen visited England in May 1961 the EFTA negotiations were already in their final stage, while in October of the same year he went to Canada and the United States, countries outside both EFTA and EEC, but where Kekkonen could enlarge on the success of Finnish policy, indicating that Finland might at some future date, always bearing in mind the need to safeguard Soviet *trade* interests—join the EEC either as a full or as an associate member.[37] It was while Kekkonen was holidaying in Hawaii that the Soviet foreign minister, Andrei Gromyko, handed the Finnish ambassador in Moscow on 30 October the note which ushered in the crisis of Finnish-Soviet relations known as the 'note crisis'.

The Soviet note[38] referred to the growing military strength of West Germany and stated that, in contradiction to the earlier-expressed attitude of Chancellor Adenauer, the Germans now wished to possess the hydrogen-bomb. The note mentioned the continuance of Nazi traditions in the Bundeswehr and the Soviet belief that Bundeswehr generals now directed NATO policy. Above all, the note expressed Soviet apprehensions at the extension of German military activity in Norway and Denmark: bases and stores for the Germans were being built there and a joint West German-Danish Baltic command was in process of formation, which would be bound to involve Norway too. Soviet fears about the Baltic could be seen in the statement that the West German fleet was concentrating in increasing strength off Flensburg. In the light of all this, the Russians proposed that consultations be held on measures to ensure the defence of the frontiers of both countries in accordance with Article 2 of the 1948 Treaty.

Because this move has such an obvious connection with the Northern Balance and a Soviet attempt to redress that balance through exerting pressure on Finland and because the Finns were told that it was the Soviet military that wanted consultations,[39] it is still the customary Finnish attitude to interpret the whole note as being more an indication of Soviet regional policy than a sign of dissatisfaction with Finnish-Soviet relations[40] (even though the note did mention the anti-Soviet tone of a section of the Finnish press). Accordingly it is pointed out that the Soviet Union exploded a 50-megaton hydrogen-bomb shortly before the note was delivered and that the Russians had for some time been trying to warn the West Germans and NATO that it viewed with concern the growing power and aggressive intent of the West German forces. In this view, the note to Finland was therefore a means to a wider end in Soviet foreign policy.

This interpretation has much to recommend it, but in its determined playing-down of the specifically 'Finnish' features in the note and 'note crisis' it does a disservice to the understanding of the fundamental problems of Finnish-Soviet relations. In 1962 a presidential election was to be held in Finland and Kekkonen's re-election was to be opposed by the candidature of Olavi Honka, a jurist without political experience, who was selected as a figure 'above party politics' by the Conservatives and Social Democrats—then still under the influence of the Tannerite group. This candidature was attacked in the Soviet press, though the note did not refer to Honka as such. At the height of the 'note crisis' Honka withdrew his candidature, presumably to prevent a worsening of Finnish-Soviet relations. Many of his supporters even went so far as to believe that Kekkonen himself had actually arranged the Soviet note so as to be sure of winning the presidential election.

This naïve viewpoint not merely underestimated the strength of the pro-Kekkonen forces in the country—he would have been elected anyway—but ignored a very basic feature of the note and the crisis round it. The Russians had come to rely on Kekkonen as their anchor-man and the genuineness of Soviet feeling towards him was expressed not only personally by Khrushchev but also by the president of the Soviet Presidium, Leonid Brezhnev, who came on a visit to Finland a few weeks before the note was delivered. Kekkonen was the bourgeois leader who was trusted by the Soviet authorities to rally the forces of his country to support both the letter and spirit of the 1948 Treaty. And this treaty was directed against a threat of attack from Germany. But now at the height of the third Berlin crisis Kekkonen had chosen to pay a visit to North America where he successfully boosted the idea of Finnish neutrality. It may be argued that the visit was arranged before the Berlin crisis, and to have backed out might have laid the president open to the suspicion of being under Soviet pressure. But what was more important, the image of Finland in the West or the maintenance of relations of confidence with the Soviet Union?

When the American historian Marvin Rintala pointed out in a talk given to the Anglo-Finnish Society in London in October 1970 that Kekkonen should have been at home and not in Hawaii at the time the note was delivered, the official Finnish representative then present angrily objected to Rintala's implication that there was a failure of Finnish foreign policy here.[41] In the actual note itself there is a reminder to the Finns, however, that Finland fought against Hitlerite Germany (i.e. in 1944-5) and that the Germans burnt down the town of Rovaniemi in Northern Finland. This, the note continued, should be 'a serious warning to those who now—consciously or *unwittingly*—close their eyes to the threatening danger from a revived German militarism and revanchism' (my italics). Germany both in Northern Europe and in the Baltic was directly threatening the security of Finland. It may be objected that the word 'unwittingly' cannot be understood as referring to Kekkonen, for the Soviet Union has never given the slightest indication that it might feel that confidence in Kekkonen was waning. But this, of course, it can hardly do, for to express a lack of confidence in Kekkonen would be to undermine the whole of the balance by which Soviet-Finnish affairs are regulated. The Soviet Union depends on Kekkonen—a dependence he was able to exploit in the crisis.

Yet his own words to the Finnish people when the crisis was resolved show the essential truth of the viewpoint that the Soviet Union did indeed have doubts about the direction of Finnish policy. By going to Novosibirsk to meet Khrushchev Kekkonen, preceded by his foreign minister, Ahti Karjalainen, succeeded in persuading the Soviet Union to agree to postpone the requested consultations. To the Finnish people Kekkonen put the matter in terms of a bargain: either the Soviet Union had faith in the Finnish political leadership, parliament, government, and president, or they would ask for the activation of the treaty. From this it may be concluded—especially in the light of the persistent warnings the Russians had given the Finns over the previous four years about West Germany—that when the Soviet Union had asked for consultations under the treaty, this had been in part at least due to a certain absence of confidence in the Finnish political leadership, parliament, government and president. For the Soviet Union 'the alignment of forces' in a bourgeois society is very fluid; perhaps the gulf between Honka and Kekkonen had not been quite as deep as the Soviet Union had wished.

The 'note crisis' of 1961 confirmed the importance of the 1948 Treaty for Finnish foreign policy. As Kekkonen said, the Soviet Union and Finland were henceforward to 'watch together' to see if there was a threat of aggression from Germany or its allies (Article 2). For while Finnish foreign policy had been concerning itself with proclaiming to the West the validity of a Finnish neutrality based on an adherence to the 1948 Treaty, the Russians' own interest had been precisely with the matter at the heart of the treaty—security against Germany. Kekkonen, who had overlooked this vital matter, was now given a reminder by the Soviet Union about it. In then making a necessary adjustment to the Russians, Kekkonen felt obliged to say that the sword of Damocles over Finland was the threat of war as a result of the worsening situation that had risen in connection with Germany and Northern Europe. For Finland, he went on, the sword of Damocles was not the Soviet note itself. But that was not how public opinion really saw the matter.

In the end, with Kekkonen's personal reassurances, and, after he had dissolved parliament and called new elections, Finnish-Soviet relations became stronger than ever (so, too, did Kekkonen's position in Finland). In 1962 the Finnish armed forces received, with the ready permission of the Soviet Union (and the more cautiously-conceded permission of the British), guided missiles.

The two crises in Finnish-Soviet relations of 1958 and 1961 show the existence of some degree of Finlandization (see below, pp. 45–9), but—and this is of far greater importance—they also show that there was a certain absence of common identity between Finnish and Soviet policy. Their respective foreign policies had some difficulty in synchronizing with each other. This is a natural product of independence in both foreign policies. At the conclusion of—and even during—both crises the statesmen of the two countries expressed a constant willingness to reach accord and to collaborate together in the future. Did Finland, after having received from the Soviet Union reminders about its internal politics and external policy, now begin to lose its independence of outlook in foreign policy? The evidence suggests that this has not happened and that Finland has gone on to pursue a foreign policy of great complexity, occasionally marred by gaffes, but more commonly subtle to a degree that has led one of its practitioners to call it Byzantine.

The essence of this Byzantinism has been the Finnish ability to work with the Soviet Union, so as to exploit Soviet démarches in Finland's own interests. Whereas up to 1961 Finnish policy seemed often to be motivated by an attempt to establish a certain distance between itself and the Soviet Union and in this way secure independence of action, after 1961 the Finns have sought to secure their ends through closer cooperation with Russia.

The 'note crisis' of 1961 was thus the dividing-line for postwar Finnish foreign policy. Since then Finland has not been used as a pawn by the Soviet Union in international crises and in consequence the implementation of the 1948 Treaty, so feared by the Finns, has not been in question. In going on to pursue an independent policy of their own, the Finns have nevertheless borne prominently in mind the nuclear danger for Northern Europe raised in the note. But their treatment of this problem, which is indeed in the forefront of Finnish foreign policy nowadays, is very different from the manner in which the issue was raised in the note. Without wanting to under-value any more the Soviet fear of German militarism, the Finns have still tried to put the nuclear question in particular into a wider framework in which the essential relationship is between the Soviet Union and the United States. This and allied matters will be dealt with more fully in the third chapter.

Notes

1. For this and other basic information about Finland see J. L. Irwin, *The Finns and the Lapps* (Newton Abbot, 1973).
2. J. Gronow, *Monopolisoituminen ja suuryhtiöden hallinta* (Helsinki, 1973), pp. 172–5.
3. The SKDL proclaims its belief in religious freedom and the separation of church from state (*Yhteishyvä*, no. 43, 24 Oct 1974).
4. J. Nousiainen, *The Finnish political system* (Cambridge, Mass., 1971), pp. 357–9.
5. E. Lyytinen, *Finland in British politics in World War I and its aftermath* (Oxford, D. Phil. diss., Sept 1973), pp. 168–9, 177.
6. K. Wahlbäck, *Mannerheimista Kekkoseen* (Porvoo-Helsinki, 1967), p. 188.
7. The opinion of M. Rintala, *Four Finns* (Berkeley, 1969), p. 108, that 'Paasikivi never changed his attitude to Russia once it was formed during his student years' cannot be accepted.
8. V. V. Pohlebkin, *Suomi vihollisena ja ystävänä* (Porvoo-Helsinki, 1969), pp. 271–4; J. Komissarov, *Suomi löytää linjansa* (Helsinki, 1974), pp. 45–6.
9. On the acrimonious dispute between two of Finland's leading historians on this question, see *Historiallinen aikakauskirja* (Helsinki, 1958), pp. 338–45, and 1959, pp. 14–21.
10. Finnish fear of and hostility to the Soviet state in the pre-1939 period is dealt with by K. Korhonen, *Naapurit vastoin tahtoaan* (Helsinki, 1966), esp. pp. 45–6, 100–4, and 205–6, and *Turvallisuuden pettäessä* (Helsinki, 1971), pp. 93–103.
11. M. Jakobson, *The diplomacy of the Winter War* (Cambridge, Mass., 1961), p. 73.
12. J. Nevakivi, *Apu jota ei pyydetty* (Helsinki, 1972), esp. ch. 9; M. Häikiö, *Suomi Englannin politiikassa vuonna 1939* (Helsinki, lic. thesis, 1971), pp. 11–121.
13. H. Jalanti, *Suomi puristuksessa* (Helsinki, 1966), pp. 356–8.
14. V. Assarsson, *Stalinin varjossa* (Porvoo-Helsinki, 1963), pp. 45–6, 54–5, and 64–5.
15. C. L. Lundin, *Finland in the Second World War* (Bloomington, 1957); A. F. Upton, *Finland in crisis 1940–1* (London, 1964).
16. For text see J. H. Wuorinen, *A history of Finland* (New York, 1965), pp. 505ff.
17. G. F. Kennan, 'Europe's problems, Europe's choices', *Foreign Policy*, 14 (1974).
18. J. O. Söderhjelm, *Kolme matkaa Moskovaan* (Tampere, 1970), pp. 98–100, and 133.
19. T. Heikkilä, *Paasikivi peräsimessä* (Helsinki, 1965), p. 307; Söderhjelm, pp. 174–5.
20. For text see Wuorinen, pp. 519ff.
21. *Ylioppilaslehti* (Helsinki), 10 Dec 1965.

22. K. Korhonen, 'Suomen puolueettomuuspolitiikka presidentti Kekkosen kaudella', in *Suomi toisen maailmansodan jälkeen*, ed. T. Perko (Turku, 1973), p. 19.
23. Apart from the argumentation of Hyvärinen and Korhonen, see also B. Broms, *Suomen puolueettomuus ja Pariisin rauhansopimuksen sekä YYA:n sotilaspoliittiset määräykset* (offprint from *Parivartio*) and J. K. Paasikivi's own statement to the Finnish people of 9 Apr 1948 in *Paasikiven linja*, vol. i (Porvoo-Helsinki, 1956), pp. 98–101.
24. On these matters the minister of the interior at that time, the Communist Y. Leino, has written in his *Kommunisti sisäministerinä*, which was intended for sale in 1958 but was withdrawn after differences among the Finnish political parties at the time of 'the night-frost crisis'. On this see also O. Leino, *Kuka oli Yrjö Leino* (Helsinki, 1973), p. 286. The sobering account written by A. Upton, *Kommunismi Suomessa* (Helsinki, 1970), pp. 214–23, is essential reading on the rumours of coups in March–April 1948.
25. *New Times*, 39 (1955).
26. Wahlbäck, *Mannerheimista Kekkoseen*, p. 211.
27. D. Anckar, *Partiopinioner och utrikespolitik* (Åbo, 1971), pp. 82–5.
28. Upton, *Kommunismi Suomessa*, pp. 272–6.
29. H. Tiainen, *Kun puolue räjähti* (Helsinki, 1968), pp. 116–17.
30. Tiainen, p. 103, criticized his own party and other forces in Finland for desiring to abandon the Paasikivi Line.
31. Wahlbäck, *Mannerheimista Kekkoseen*, p. 211.
32. N. S. Hruštšev (Khrushchev), *Neuvostoliitto ja Pohjola* (Helsinki, 1964), p. 58.
33. Ibid., p. 50.
34. Kekkonen quoted Paasikivi's actions as a precedent in his broadcast on 10 Dec 1958. On Paasikivi's warning the press, see Heikkilä, pp. 91–6.
35. Hruštšev, pp. 79–80, 83–4, 121–3, and 132.
36. In November 1960 Khrushchev (Hruštšev, p. 135) expressed his understanding of the Finnish need to enter into a special arrangement with EFTA that would protect Finnish trading interests with the West.
37. Remarks made in a press interview of 17 Oct 1961, *UPLA*, 1961, p. 139.
38. *Soviet News*, 31 Oct 1961.
39. N. J. Thögersen, *De finske-sovjetiske relationer* (Åhus, lic. thesis, Dec 1969), p. 118.
40. e.g. L. A. Puntila, 'Suomen kansainvälisen aseman kehitys toisen maailmansodan jälkeen', in *Suomen ulkopolitiikan kehityslinjat 1809–1966*, ed. I. Hakalehto (Porvoo-Helsinki, 1966), pp. 129–32.
41. M. Rintala, *A foreigner looks at Finland's foreign policy*, talk given at the Anglo-Finnish Society, London, 6 Oct 1970.

FROM this brief review of Finnish history it is at once apparent that, in contrast to the main prewar trend in policy—a tendency to avoid any commitment to the powers, which led to the isolation of Finland in the Winter War—Finnish postwar policy has been based on an acknowledgement of a great power political interest. This interest happens to be the security interests of the Soviet Union. But though it would be heresy nowadays to say so in Finland, the real roots of this policy stem from the commitment to Germany in 1941, the point at which Finnish leaders felt that participation in the disturbing world of great power politics was unavoidable. Paasikivi's career illustrates this conviction. Having been sympathetic to the Germans in 1940–1, he nevertheless led his fellow countrymen in 1944 to accept once more the necessity of recognizing Russia's security interests in Finland as a condition of Finland's survival as a state. Thus Paasikivi, a Conservative, who was chairman of his party from 1934–6, a banker and a director of one of Finland's largest banks (the Kansallis-Osake-Pankki) from 1934–6, showed himself to be an outstanding opportunist in foreign policy, like many statesmen, although the simplified Paasikivi *persona* now projected by Finnish and Soviet publicists is that of a patriot who understood Russian security needs. Paasikivi's real legacy to his fellow countrymen was his commitment to an understanding of the basic realities of power politics. In this sense, despite the ideological differences that separate them from Paasikivi's Conservatism, the young Leftists Blomberg, Joenniemi, the brothers Kalela, and others[1] who advocate that Finns must recognize the need for military and political cooperation in a conflict situation with the Soviet Union are in the true Paasikivi Line.

Paasikivi was not of course the only Finnish statesman to realize the truth—a rather complex one as it turned out—that Finland had to come to terms with the *Realpolitik* of the great powers. The most ardent propagandist of the Continuation War was a politician who wrote under the pen-name of Pekka Peitsi (Peter the Lance). This man, who urged his countrymen to make the greatest of sacrifices in the war against the Soviet Union, had characteristically been one of the three members of parliament who had voted against the peace terms of the Winter War, and therefore felt an overwhelming personal conviction of the need for Finland to trust in and profit from the power of the Wehrmacht. Pekka Peitsi's real name was Urho Kekkonen, who by 1943 was advocating a switch in Finnish policy towards an accommodation with the Soviet Union and who, as minister of justice from 17 November 1944 to 26 March 1946, was responsible for the prosecution of the 'war criminals' who a few years earlier had led his country to war alongside Nazi Germany. This latter act, undertaken in the light of the requirements of Article 23 of the armistice agreement and with the approval of Paasikivi, then prime minister, earned for Kekkonen the opprobrium of many of his fellow countrymen, who were additionally incensed by his supposedly close relations with the Soviet minister Pavel Orlov.[2] Kekkonen survived in political life and went on to become prime minister in the 50s (from 17 March 1950 to 17 November 1953 and from 20 October 1954 to 3 March 1956) and president in 1956, a post he still retains. As president he has become a high priest of firm relations of security and friendship with the Soviet Union, so that for well over a decade it has been customary to speak of a Paasikivi-Kekkonen Line in Finnish foreign policy, the one a natural continuation of the other. The crowning-point of the several shifts in Kekkonen's political outlook is his identification with the viewpoint that, by virtue of the Finnish-Soviet security relationship, Finland's international position is now unquestionably secure and above all speculation.[3]

Hand in hand with this belief goes the rejection of prewar and wartime policy. In a speech given at Kouvola in eastern Finland on 28 December 1961, Kekkonen publicly stated that in the prewar world 'we did not at all understand the importance of foreign policy and its requirements'. This, he went on to say, should make Finns look critically at their past: 'How can we lead the fortunes of our country in a happier direction if we fail to study its past and see what was wrong with it?'

It must again be emphasized that these opinions should not be allowed to obscure the fact that a total rejection of prewar thinking on foreign policy would be unusual in a state that managed to retain the essence of its prewar political system. If, as is argued here, the fundamental change in Finnish thinking about foreign policy came with the decision to join Germany in the invasion of Russia in 1941 —when Finland, in short, at last came to terms with great power

2

politics—we must note that this change was not a total one. For Finland went to war not as an ally but as a co-belligerent of Germany. This viewpoint expressed Finland's *limited* involvement in the war: indeed, Jakobson, in the wisdom of hindsight, has even seen this as a kind of neutrality.[4] In this way Finnish wartime policy retained a part of its prewar policy—an aspiration not to be dragged down by involvement with the great powers. Certain Finnish wartime actions, such as the decision not to bomb the Murmansk railway, the Allied lifeline to the Soviet Union, seem to indicate a desire on the part of the Finns to communicate to the Allies that Finland was not entirely in the Axis camp. In fact, there was something different about Finland from the Allied point of view. The Americans did not declare war on the Finns and Churchill at Teheran tried to put in a good word for them.[5] When the armistice came, the Russians trusted the Finns to expel the Germans and thus Soviet troops were spared for service in the main theatre of operations against Germany.

At the end of the war both the Finnish president, Marshal Gustav Mannerheim, and the Finnish head of the defence forces, General Aarne Sihvo, spoke of entering into a security arrangement with the Soviet Union, although Sihvo's attitude was probably more genuine than Mannerheim's, since the latter was inveigled by Andrei Zhdanov into making an admission about this matter. Perhaps it was Paasikivi who in this period more closely expressed the underlying Finnish attitude to this delicate question when he wrote, in an article published on 10 February 1947, that Finland would never allow a foreign power to invade its territory en route to Russia. This unilateral promise recalled the prewar statements of Finnish leaders, who reassured Boris Yartsev and other Soviet emissaries that Finland would fight if the Germans tried to invade Russia through Finnish territory but did not wish to enter into a written agreement to this effect with Russia, involving Russian aid.

Once the 1948 Treaty was signed, the original Soviet text having been much amended by the Finns in the negotiations, Paasikivi hurried to tell his nation in a radio broadcast on 9 April 1948 that the obligations incurred by Finland under the treaty had been limited as narrowly as possible. The aspiration of Finland, expressed in the preamble of the treaty, 'to remain outside the conflicting interests of the Great Powers' was originally phrased by Paasikivi in terms of an aspiration to be 'outside international conflicts of interest'—which would actually have been contradictory to the main purpose of the treaty, a defence against a revived and aggressive Germany.[6] In any case this statement in the preamble was later used by the Finns themselves as an endorsement of Finnish neutrality, an opinion to which one Soviet commentator, the so-called Yuri Komissarov, at least takes strong exception,[7] for his government has not endorsed it in this way. This Finnish aspiration clearly harks back to the pre-war desire to seek withdrawal from potential conflict situations.

Finally, it is important to note that immediately before and during the actual treaty negotiations with the Soviet Union the Finnish government expressed its concern to the representatives of the United States, Britain, France, and Sweden. This was done with the cognizance of Paasikivi.[8]

All these facts show that while Finland does feel able to enter into a security arrangement with one power, it does not want to go so far as to have that power regarded as its ally. The relationship with an ally might be too close and lead to the reduction of Finland to a satellite status. In addition, it is clear that the Finns want to keep their channels open to all the powers. In this connection the important factor is that Finland is a West European state, ideologically, culturally, and as we shall see in chapter 4—in large measure also economically, bound to the West.

However, the West cannot offer Finland security; it is geographically too remote and its proffered aid, as in the latter stages of the Winter War in 1940, might aggravate the situation rather than assist the Finns. The fundamental problem has been that, as far as the traditionalist political thinking of the Finnish educated élite has been concerned, the West was unfortunately divided along the broad lines of Britain, France, and the United States versus Germany. This political division has been viewed with regret by many Finns of the older generation, who felt an affinity with the West as a whole and wanted to regard what they themselves called 'the great culture lands' (a term that excluded Russia) as a unity. The two world wars were an obvious denial of this unity, but the destruction of German power in 1945 appeared drastically to simplify the overall situation in Europe. There were now only two forces in Europe, the West and the Soviet Union.

A number of prominent Finnish officers believed that the West and the Soviet Union might soon come into conflict. For this eventuality a series of arms caches were laid down from September 1944—the preliminary decision to do so being made in early August—to the spring of 1945 in various parts of Finland. (It has been somewhat less convincingly argued that this arms caching was also done in the light of possible difficulties in expelling German forces from Finnish soil.) In any case the officers involved were prosecuted by the Finnish state authorities for preparing illegal armed activity, among the accused being General A. F. Airo, the former chief of general staff, but the case against him was ultimately dropped.[9]

The outlook that inspired these men—and which Paasikivi and Kekkonen regarded as disastrous for Finland[10]—did not simply wither away with their prosecution. A feeling that in its security policy the West should not neglect Finland has continued to haunt the fundamental thinking of some bourgeois circles in the country. It is interesting to note that when some years ago the American futurologist Herman Kahn stated that Finland was outside the area of protective concern of American security policy, there were expressions of bitterness in several Finnish newspapers. In an article published on 11 May 1969—several months later—the *Helsingin Sanomat* described him as the 'writer off of Finland'.

Be that as it may, the fact is that in postwar Finland two more important ways of thinking about the country's foreign-political position have triumphed. The most far-ranging of these is Kekkonen's. When still actually writing under the pseudonym of Pekka Peitsi, as early as 1944 he put forward a blueprint for Finland's position in the postwar world. Unlike the officers who buried caches of arms, Kekkonen, who as minister of justice was to demand severe punishment for these officers, did not believe that the two power camps of the West and the Soviet Union would come into conflict with each other: on the contrary, he was convinced that their wartime cooperation indicated that they were influencing each other in a positive fashion. The most outstanding example of this influence was the spread of what he called 'the social way of thinking' in England and even America, a phenomenon he saw as being due in part to an appreciation in those countries of the level of social security attained in the USSR. To a degree, therefore, Kekkonen was putting forward a mild kind of convergence theory. Because the two power camps were approaching each other in these ways, there would be good grounds in the postwar world for the emergence of a system of collective security, in which the small states too would have their place. But small states had to adapt themselves to this process and scheme of things. Finland must put its own house in order by radicalizing itself. This process of radicalization, part of something that was going to take place all over Europe, would have the particular significance for Finland of forming the basic pre-condition for cooperation with the Soviet Union, which was the essential change that had to be made in Finland's foreign policy.[11]

Paasikivi, on the other hand, had a much more restrained view of his country's position in the postwar world. A Conservative, on the Right of his Party if anything, he was hardly in a position to welcome the 'radicalization' of Finnish life that Kekkonen, a bourgeois politician of the Centre (the Agrarian Union—a farmers' party) seemed to welcome. Nevertheless he too believed in internal changes. They were a necessity, because 'we are a conquered country', as he told a complaining party delegation.[12] In short, it was not the general nature of the postwar world Finland had to adjust to: it was the intrusive presence of the Soviet Union, whose commands were expressed in the armistice agreement and whose power was dominant in the Control Commission in the person of Andrei Zhdanov and later in the Soviet minister Pavel Orlov. The power reality for Paasikivi was the Soviet Union, and because of this simple fact he kept the Finnish press in order, suppressed 'Fascist' movements such as the Aseveliliitto ('Brothers-in-Arms Union'—a largely Social Democratic patriotic organization), insisted on the trial of some of Finland's most respected leaders on charges of war guilt, and put the SKDL into the government, where they supplied the prime minister in the person of Mauno Pekkala (a former Social Democrat) and the minister of the interior in the person of Yrjö Leino (a Communist).

The internal changes that occurred in Finland during the years 1944–8 must be seen first of all from the point of view of the form in which they occurred. In that light it will be seen that a society succeeded in defending itself. At the top, an ailing and increasingly depressed aristocratic president, Marshal Mannerheim, who held office from 4 August 1944 to 3 April 1946, nevertheless by his mere presence in office helped the patriotic and conservative forces to stand firm. The stiffening was supplied by Paasikivi, first as prime minister and then as president. As president, with the direction of foreign policy in his hands, and also as commander-in-chief of the armed forces—both powers decreed by the constitution—Paasikivi could endure a Popular Front government, where in any case the SKDL were balanced by the Social Democrats and Agrarians and where the prime minister, Mauno Pekkala, though a member of the SKDL, was trusted as one who would not disturb the country's economic system.[13]

In the meantime the war leaders had been tried by the Finns themselves in order to forestall any action by the Soviet Union: none of them was sentenced to death, though the Finnish Communist leader Hertta Kuusinen demanded death sentences for some of them. The maximum sentence was of ten years' hard labour passed on the former president Risto Ryti, who had held office from 19 December 1940 until 1 August 1944.

However, the changes that occurred in the immediate postwar years certainly did represent some radicalization of Finnish society and politics. The Finnish trade union movement, which had been under something of a cloud in the prewar years (when unionism was actually forbidden in many factories) trebled its membership after the war,[14] though as a matter of fact trade unionism had been growing during the war, being encouraged by the authorities as part of the integration of workers in the war effort. And the general tolerance for the Left that was now evident in Finnish life inevitably helped the growth of the trade union movement. But the most obvious sign of the radicalization of Finnish life was the emergence into legality of the Finnish Communist Party and the willingness of both the Social Democrats and Agrarians to participate in governments with the Communists. A Popular Front government was in office until July 1948 and the memory of this government has much significance for the Centre and the Left, for the Popular Front government was reborn in 1966 and, with one short break, continued until 1971. It is this type of government that is the clearest expression of radicalism in Finland, a radicalism that is political and social and has not yet dared to tamper with the country's basic economic structure.

The legalization of the extreme Left meant their endorsement of parliamentary ways and, where possible, participation in parliamentary government. This integration involved their containment, the source of a problem for the Finnish Communist Party that has come to the fore in recent years with the development of a hardline 'Stalinist' wing in the party that has found little gain for the proletariat in the Popular Front governments of 1966–71 and does not wish for further Communist participation in a government of this kind. It should be noted that the integration of the Communist Party into Finnish life has now gone so far that the Communist leader Hertta Kuusinen appeared in recent years on TV chat shows and in January 1969 the Conservatives expressed their willingness in principle to consider entering a government which included Communists. Communists are to be found occupying many important posts in the civil service and they sit on innumerable official committees and boards in proportion to their parliamentary strength. Among other things, this means that they sit on the Parliamentary Foreign Affairs Committee. On the other hand Communists have not been admitted to the Foreign Office—and the apparent exception made with the appointment of Reino Paasilinna to the post of Information Officer at the Moscow Embassy was disproved in a *Helsingin Sanomat* article of 19 January 1975 sympathetic to Paasilinna that denied his membership of any party, though his outlook seems to be that of the extreme Left. Communists continue to be kept out—even in military service—of the Officers' School, as the Communist vice-president of the Finnish trade union movement maintained in the spring of 1974.[15] The latter fact provides an interesting comment on the need felt in the Finnish armed forces to keep ideological factors out of any cooperation with the Soviet Union that might be enjoined in a crisis situation by the 1948 Treaty. This exclusion of Communists is a natural consequence of the existence of a Finnish dilemma.

The integration of the Communists into Finnish society has been partial in another sense, for the creation of the SKDL leftist front in 1944 did not lead to the absorption of the Social Democratic Party which, after many vicissitudes, has gradually strengthened its position. This party, after the Finnish civil war of 1918, had kept alive the idea of a constitutionalist and anti-insurrectionist socialism, and as early as 1926 formed a government for a year, thereafter playing an important role in the coalition government that was in office when Finland entered the Winter War. During the two wars it took a strongly patriotic line against the Soviet Union and its leader Väinö Tanner was jailed as a war criminal. The party became divided in the postwar years on its attitude to cooperation with the Communists: some members like Mauno Pekkala joined the SKDL, others like K. A. Fagerholm initially supported cooperation with the Communists and SKDL, still others became increasingly fearful of such cooperation and remembered with pride the patriotism of wartime days. The toughening attitude of communist parties in Western Europe enjoined upon them by Zhdanov at the Cominform meeting of September 1947[16] also had its repercussions on the relations between the Communists and Social Democrats in Finland. The belief, however vague the evidence for it was, that a section at least of the Communists had contemplated a coup in the spring of 1948 and the demand to keep the post of minister of the interior in their hands put forward by the SKDL in the government discussions in the summer of 1948 confirmed for most Social Democrats the untrustworthiness of cooperation with the extreme Left. In July Fagerholm, now disillusioned, formed a minority Social Democrat government that lasted until March 1950.

The existence of this government precipitated a crisis in Finnish-Soviet relations, for the Fagerholm cabinet was accused of trying to swing Finland round to 'Third Force' ideas, and the appearance in Finland during this time of emissaries from the Western trade union movement in the person of Victor Feather of the TUC and the bitterly anti-Communist William Green of the AFL[17] further darkened the picture both for the Soviet Union and, as it turned out, for the Social Democrats. With Soviet commentators now openly attacking the Paasikivi Line,[18] Paasikivi in 1950 dropped the Social Democrats and put the Agrarians in under the premiership of Urho Kekkonen.

Thereafter the strange tacit alliance between the Agrarians and the Soviet Union began gradually to develop. The Social Democrats did in fact participate in several of the governments of the 50s, but as the Left continued to be divided and as Väinö Tanner (released from jail in 1949) was elected chairman of the party in 1957, Soviet dislike of the Social Democrats did not abate. They became more and more associated in the Soviet mind with a pro-Western foreign policy based on the anti-Soviet patriotism of the war years. Thus in coming to terms with a bourgeois state, the Russians found their point of support in that state in a bourgeois party, the Agrarians, since 1965 the Centre Party.

This party, a party of farmers, which communism extinguished in Eastern Europe, was acceptable in a Finnish context to the Soviet leaders because it was not a party of large capital, though through the wood and paper industry it had links with the Right. The Agrarian Party, in spite of the personal ruthlessness and arrogance of many of its leaders, was a very flexible party, with the possibility of entering into relations with both Left and Right. It was an intensely Finnish party that owed little to ideological inspirations from without, and it did not have the international contacts of the larger capitalists on the one hand and the Social Democrats on the other. To this day the Centre Party is embarrassed by no equivalent of the Socialist International, where at the Helsinki meeting in 1971 a Finnish Social Democratic leader got up and serenaded Golda Meir. Internally the

Centre, except in certain rural areas, do not openly seem to compete with the Communists or SKDL for votes, as the Social Democrats certainly do. It is in the Agrarian Centre Party, a party after all of property, that Finnish bourgeois society as a whole has best been able to defend itself.

The power of the weak

Finland's first service to the Soviet Union occurred during the war when it agreed to expel the German forces as a condition of the armistice. There was thus no excuse for a large body of Soviet troops to be in the country, and by this deal Finland escaped Soviet occupation forces. It then continued to serve Soviet interests by committing itself to oppose a future German invasion of the Soviet Union through Finnish territory (1948 Treaty). Since Finland would anyway only be a secondary route for such an invasion (the main thrust coming through the Northern Tier of Poland and Czechoslovakia), Russia had no need to precipitate a takeover of Finland, even though Zhdanov is later said to have felt that it should have done this, and a successful Finnish Communist attempt in this direction would inevitably have been welcome to the Soviet Union. In the event, the Soviet authorities contented themselves by adopting a bargaining stance with the Finns: if the Finns adhered to the treaty, they would be left alone by the Russians. A certain balance of dependence, to use one of J. Galtung's terms,[19] thus developed in the Finnish-Soviet relationship. Of course the Soviet Union had the power to overwhelm the Finns, but once they settled for a balance of dependence the Finns too could exert power. This came out clearly at the time of the negotiations for the treaty when Molotov wanted to be reassured that the Finnish parliament would ratify it, a factor that may have helped the Finnish negotiators to get through the vital emendations to Stalin's original draft.

With the evident failure by the end of 1949 of the Zhdanov hard line and the corresponding change in Soviet policy towards a cultivation of new tactics, such as the 'peace offensive', the conditions for Finnish bargaining power improved. The question began to turn more and more upon neutrality and what it meant both for the Soviet Union and Finland. In the early days of the peace campaign the doctrine of neutrality still remained suspect: 'there could be no neutrality in the struggle for peace'. Soviet analyses of

Swedish neutrality—a phenomenon of great significance for Finland—continued for some time to represent the Swedish position as hypocritical: Sweden had accepted Marshall Aid and so was obviously pro-Western in outlook.[20] In Finland, too, according to the Soviet commentator, A. Kornilov, reactionary forces, including the Tannerite pro-Western Social Democrats, were exploiting the phrase in the preamble to the 1948 Treaty about Finland's remaining outside power conflicts, so as to produce a dubious neutrality that was clearly serving Western interests.[21] The veteran Finnish Communist leader in exile in the Soviet Union, O. W. Kuusinen (the father of Hertta Kuusinen and a member of the Soviet politburo) gave this a slightly different emphasis: if Finland became really determined, the West would leave it alone and the principle of staying outside power conflicts would become a reality.[22] This was a tacit endorsement of the possibilities of Finnish neutrality.

For the Soviet Union, which tried to exploit its own declared neutrality at the time of the Korean War, states which claimed to be genuinely neutral could be seen to some extent to counteract the influence of blocs, i.e. the NATO security system. In Finland neutrality, in the mouths of the Western-orientated Social Democrats, was obviously suspect. But Kekkonen and his Agrarians were a different matter.

On 23 January 1952 the first important postwar Finnish foreign political démarche was made. This was the plan, drawn up by Prime Minister Kekkonen, with President Paasikivi's approval and scrutiny, contained in Kekkonen's so-called 'pyjama speech'—a speech he never delivered owing to illness, but being convalescent, pulled out of his pyjama pocket and gave to the press. In this speech Kekkonen advocated the creation of 'a neutral alliance between the Scandinavian countries'. Since the Soviet Union had come down heavily against a Nordic Defence Alliance that had been mooted at the end of 1948, this being from the Soviet point of view a mere front for Western penetration ('the bridgehead theory'),[23] it was bold of Paasikivi and Kekkonen to propose another Nordic scheme that would involve by definition military cooperation among the Nordic states. But in the 'pyjama speech' care was taken to emphasize that the 1948 Treaty with the Soviet Union would not be upset by any new Nordic arrangements: on the contrary, these arrangements would form 'a logical conclusion' to the treaty, for a defence alliance of Northern neutrals 'would remove even the theoretical threat of an attack on the USSR via Finland's territory'. At the same time, of course, Finland's security position—so obviously one-sided—would be balanced from the West (i.e. against the East).

The initial Social Democrat reaction to this plan was one of flustered anger, for they believed that it was really aimed at NATO and they thus regarded it as being contrary to true neutrality, as set forth in the preamble to the 1948 Treaty. In fact, Kekkonen, as he confessed in a letter to the leading Social Democrat, Emil Skog, was trying in this proposal to counteract the attempts of the former Danish prime minister, H. C. Hedtoft, to draw Sweden away from its policy of neutrality. In attempting to bolster up Swedish neutrality by his plan, Kekkonen claimed that he was safeguarding Finnish interests, for if Sweden changed its neutral policy, then 'so much the worse for us'—in short a change in Swedish policy would mean an intensification of Russian control in Finland. This was a use by Kekkonen of the Northern Balance concept (see p. 39).

The Soviet Union rose to the bait and expressed approval of the Finnish démarche 'to refuse to have any part in the aggressive Atlantic Pact, to observe strict neutrality'. This was one of the earliest of Soviet acknowledgements of Finnish neutrality.[24] The perceptive Finnish Social Democrat journalist, Arvo Tuominen (a former Communist), writing from the vantage-point of Stockholm, saw that a Finnish and Soviet interest had happily coincided in the plan and that this worked to the benefit of Nordic neutrality and Finnish sovereignty.[25]

Of course Norway and Denmark did not leave NATO, but the Swedes did not abandon neutrality either, though it can hardly be assumed that this was due to the Kekkonen-Paasikivi plan. The démarche was assuredly one of those measures that could scarcely expect realization but was important none the less in the context of Finnish-Soviet relations. By 1955 Finland was being vociferously praised by Soviet commentators for its 'non-participation in military blocs', which was bound to have a favourable influence on 'neutralist forces' elsewhere in Scandinavia.[26] No wonder that in that year the Soviet Union saw no objection to Finnish membership of the Nordic Council (established to promote cooperation between Scandinavian parliaments and governments). Happiest of all, at the turn of the year Soviet forces were withdrawn from the Porkkala base, near Helsinki, an act which Paasikivi himself regarded as the removal of the final impediment to Finnish neutrality.

Problems raised by the 1948 Treaty

Finland's history clearly shows that in *Finnish* terms the problem of relations with Russia has always been the threat of absorption, so that the distinctive Finnish way of life would be lost for ever. This possibility, as we have seen, existed in the latter days of the Tsarist empire and in the early decades of the new Soviet state. In *Russian* terms the crux of relations with Finland was a military-strategic problem of how to defend the north-western flank of Russia, and in particular the city of St Petersburg-Leningrad—hence the 1948 Treaty. But since the Finns have neither had the power nor the interest to cherish aggressive designs (though at times they have shown a strong and active interest in East Karelia, inhabited by a kindred nation), it was difficult for them to understand Russian preoccupation with the defence of the St Petersburg-Leningrad district—a preoccupation activated by a threat from Western or, more often, Central Europe. The Finns have tended to view any preventive measures proposed by the Russians and involving the Finns themselves, in the light of a threat outside the area, as the thin end of the wedge leading to their eventual absorption. But Paasikivi during the negotiations for the 1920 peace treaty did understand the defence needs of Leningrad, and it was this that made him urge that territorial concessions should be made by Finland in the abortive discussions preceding the Winter War. It was also he who, after 1944, led his fellow countrymen once more to accept the necessity of recognizing Russia's security interests in Finland as a condition of Finland's survival as a state.

The fact that nowadays a fruitful relationship does exist between the two countries is all the more remarkable taking into account the fact that Finland has been at war with the Soviet Union twice this century (in the Winter War and Continuation War). Indeed, as has been seen, many right-wing Finns believe that their country was at war with Russia for a third time, during the civil war, which they considered to have been fought against the intrusion of Bolshevism into Finland. Certainly for the Soviet Union relations with Finland have become a sterling example of the reality of peaceful coexistence between states with different social and political systems. For their part the Finns gladly accept this view, for it is a Soviet endorsement of the Finns' right to live their own way of life. Nor is this endorsement merely passively and thankfully accepted in Finland. Within the framework of peaceful coexistence, the Finns feel that they themselves are playing a pioneer role that has some significance beyond the confines of Finnish-Soviet relations. In an interview reported in a Soviet journal in 1968 the then Finnish foreign minister, Ahti Karjalainen, expressed pride in the fact that his country was the first capitalist country to establish a fruitful relationship with the Soviet Union in the postwar world.[27] Some foreign observers have drawn parallel conclusions. David Vital, for example, sees Finland's relationship with the Soviet Union as one of the most successful cases of relations between a small and great power in the contemporary international political scene. Vital even goes so far as to say that this relationship is 'a paradigm for the future'.[28]

The fact that Finland retained its social and political system intact and had no communist takeover continued to bind the country to Northern and not to Eastern Europe. Moreover the nature of Finland's security arrangements with the Soviet Union brought Finland, gradually over the years, into a mutually complementary North European security system that has become known generally as the Northern Balance. For once Finland, by the 1948 Treaty, entered into a security relationship with the Soviet Union, it was inevitable that Norway and Denmark should seek a compensatory tie-up, which they did in 1949 by joining NATO. But the commitment to NATO of these two countries is to some extent a partial commitment—as is Finland's (in a different way) to the Soviet Union, for both Norway and Denmark have refused to have NATO bases and nuclear weapons and the Norwegians do not station troops permanently in the province of Finnmark, which borders on the Soviet Union and northern Finland. Pivoting the Northern Balance is Sweden, a well-armed neutral, bound in treaty obligation to no major power. The diverse security arrangements made by the different Northern European countries have one thing in common: they are limited arrangements, and it is this fact that has led one Norwegian commentator, to refer in an article to the existence of a 'low Northern Balance'.[29]

Another Norwegian commentator, J. J. Holst, has pointed out in the same journal[30] that the Northern Balance actually arose in a somewhat accidental way, for it was a Northern Defence Union that first absorbed the attention of Norway, Sweden, and Denmark in 1948, and only on the failure of this idea did Norway and Denmark join NATO and Sweden remain neutral. Nevertheless, from the point of view of the powers an embryonic Northern Balance seems to have developed early. Stalin regarded Norway as falling within the British and later Western sphere of influence in wartime and in the immediate postwar years:[31] the British correspondingly acted at this time as if Finland were primarily a Russian matter.[32] On the other hand the powers were easily persuaded not to view the North in terms of maximum security precautions. Indeed, Norway was left out of the first draft for a Western European Union, while the Soviet Union, originally expecting Finland to sign a treaty comparable in kind to those already concluded with Hungary and Romania, in fact rather readily accepted the initial Finnish request that the obligations of the parties be restricted to hostilities in Finland. The Northern Balance exists for the Finns by virtue of the absence of any maximum security commitment on the part of the several Northern states. This, together with the similarity of institutional life between Finland and the Nordic states, makes Finland a part of Northern, not Eastern, Europe.

Clearly the Northern European states feel that there is a certain danger in the adoption of a maximum security policy—Holst and Brundtland, for example, argue that Norway's *limited* commitment to NATO was actually made in this form to avoid arousing the suspicions of the Soviet Union. Still, the Norwegians do retain the option of increasing their NATO commitment, i.e. of receiving bases and nuclear weapons on their soil if a crisis develops. Similarly, it can be argued that the Finns, whose limited commitment to the Soviet Union does not involve them in any automatic and general military cooperation with the Warsaw Pact should a crisis in Europe occur, can nevertheless summon Soviet aid should they feel a need to strengthen their security in the light of the threat envisaged in the first two articles of the 1948 Treaty. For it is Soviet aid that is the obvious answer to resolving the contradiction between the peace treaty limitations on the size and equipment of the Finnish armed forces and the task enjoined upon them by the 1948 Treaty of repelling an attack by Germany and its allies. And the possibility of Soviet aid is set out in the first article of the treaty.

It is at this point, however, that the cluster of problems summed up in the concept of a Finnish dilemma really begins to occur. These problems in a crisis situation would be so acute that some Finnish spokesmen argue that their nation could field an army from the reserves within twenty-four hours of up to 700,000 men, a grossly exaggerated maximum figure that if acted upon would mean the immediate wrecking of the Finnish economy—something less than half this figure might be more reasonable. It is additionally argued, among others by Hyvärinen, that the possibility of Soviet aid mentioned in the treaty means material aid and not Soviet troops. Hyvärinen goes on to argue that in a general conflict situation the Soviet Union would anyway have no troops to spare for Finland. Opinions of this kind, if taken in conjunction with the Finnish argumentation about the treaty, lead to the inescapable conclusion that the real Finnish security problem (in the eyes of the leaders hitherto of Finnish society) lies precisely with the one power that, according to the treaty itself, should be helping to guarantee Finnish security, namely the Soviet Union.

The fact is that if a general European conflict occurred the Finns would find themselves, from the standpoint of their own ideological traditions and beliefs, on the wrong side by virtue of their obligations to the Soviet Union under the 1948 Treaty. In such a situation the umbrella of peaceful coexistence would have limply collapsed and the naked bond of joint military action with the Soviet Union would replace it. Thus the majority of Finns, even if loyally supporting the obligations of the treaty, cannot wish for the triumph of Soviet power in Europe, for, as the present Finnish president reminded Nikita Khrushchev in a speech delivered on 4 September 1960, the majority of the Finnish people want Finland to remain 'a traditional Scandinavian democracy' and, he added, 'we shall defend our system under all circumstances'.

In a general conflict situation in Europe the Finns would therefore be faced with a number of complex problems. How far does the very fact of having a security treaty with the Soviet Union raise expectations among the Soviet military leaders that they will be able to control Finland and move across it, through Finnish air-space, for example? And how far will this render Finland, a country that is not a member of the Warsaw Pact, liable nevertheless to be regarded to all intents and purposes as a Warsaw Pact country as far as Western military retaliation is concerned? As well as having a security treaty with the Soviet Union, Finland is also a neutral country, whose armed forces are committed, in pursuance of the maintenance of neutrality, to repel any infringements of neutrality (see the section 'A Neutral Borderland' in chapter 3). How far does this conflict with the spirit of the security treaty with the Soviet Union, whose leaders, thinking of the treaty, might assume far more than Finnish neutrality was prepared to grant them? The problem for the Finns therefore is that of being able to maintain, in the light of the reactions of both European blocs, the credibility of their own limited objectives. The dilemma that the Finns face is that the closer they come in a conflict situation to the Soviet side the more likely it is that they will simply be included in hostile action from the Western side, while on the other hand if the Soviet leaders once feel that there is anything the least unreliable in the Finnish attitude, retaliation from the Soviet side will occur.

There is a subordinate but very important dilemma arising in a situation in which it is felt that the West will try to penetrate Finland militarily. To what extent could Finland alone succeed in thwarting such attacks and at what point would the country have to accept Soviet aid, which on the one hand might be provocative to the West and on the other would bring with it the fear of a Soviet takeover of Finland?

How far could Finland in these difficult circumstances maintain some kind of relations with the West, particularly from the point of view of preserving its credibility as a distinctive state and society? How could the Finns keep open their relations with their Scandinavian fellow nations (if Sweden succeeded in remaining neutral in a conflict situation, there would then be three different security groupings in Northern Europe)? These problems are of an intolerable nature, though no one who knows the Finns would expect them to panic under their impact if a major breakdown in European relations occurred. Nevertheless this is for the Finns their own special version of 'thinking about the unthinkable' and as is customary in these matters issues are often blurred. In opposition to the traditionalist attempt to think in terms of a certain manœuverability here, some of the younger left-wing Social Democratic analysts, notably Blomberg and Joenniemi,[33] have, however, come out with a clear advocacy of the need to recognize the inescapability of cooperation with the Soviet Union in the crisis situation described in the 1948 Treaty. An earlier head of the armed forces, General Aarne Sihvo, also wished for the acknowledgement of a clear obligation to the Soviet Union, especially in view of the fact that otherwise the nation might be divided at the moment of crisis.[34]

It may, of course, be argued that the chances of a conflict occurring between the West and the Soviet Union in Europe are so remote that the Finnish dilemma will never materialize, because the happy continuance of European détente, as visualized by the present Finnish prime minister at the Finnish Pugwash Conference in 1972, is inevitable. Yet such an argument in no way diminishes the impact that consideration of the dilemma has for Finnish policy-making. For the dilemma would occur when Finland was involved in the extreme crisis situation, and it is from consideration of this extreme situation that security policy starts.[35] And other crisis situations have occurred which, though not of the most extreme kind, still did raise the spectre of the dilemma: how far to go? Thus at the time of the 1968 Czechoslovak crisis it was rumoured that for a brief period certain units of the Finnish armed forces were on the alert, a demonstrative measure taken against the Soviet Union, Kosygin's later visit to Kekkonen being regarded as a reassurance of Soviet goodwill to the Finns. On the other hand, when Western action in Norway and Denmark provoked in the 'note crisis' of 1961 a Soviet response that had negative implications in it for the Finns, it was the Finns who succeeded in demonstrating an apparent ability to manoeuvre by reassuring the Russians without entering into a commitment to military consultations with them.

The problems of the 1948 Treaty for the Finns have been dealt with in some detail by researchers working from the Stockholm Utrikespolitiska Institutet. Katarina Brodin has felt that the Finnish attitude has been to regard the treaty as positive in peacetime, but to seek to avoid a situation where Articles 1 and 2 would have to be implemented.[36] As with Krister Wahlbäck's analysis, she has considered the matter basically from the point of view of the credibility of Finnish neutrality in these circumstances. The real dilemma only begins, however, if Finland's pretensions to neutrality (to be dealt with more fully in chapter 3) lose their validity. In that case, an open conflict situation in Europe, the treaty may indeed serve the positive goal of helping to regulate relations with the USSR, a virtue that even a hostile commentator like Nils Ørvik finds the treaty has,[37] but on the other hand there exists the ever present danger that the Soviet Union, having acted on the bases the treaty provides, will henceforward ignore all Finnish viewpoints and dominate the country. The treaty therefore does not give the Finns the maximum security that mutual assistance treaties are always supposed to ensure. It may be better than having no treaty at all, but there is still a terrible risk. For this basic reason the main burden of Finnish security policy lies elsewhere: it lies in the démarches of an active foreign policy.

Security policy, much debated by the Finns in the 60s,[38] was then defined in terms of an equation: foreign policy+defence policy= security policy. This means that foreign policy is subordinated to security policy ends: at the same time the Finnish commentators stressed that it was foreign policy rather than defence policy that bore the main responsibility for the attainment of Finnish security objectives. A further point, the importance of which will be discussed in chapter 3, is that foreign policy and defence policy appear to have a certain independence from each other, so that defence policy is no longer to be considered as simply the arm of foreign policy in the sense, for example, of the definition given in the early period of Finland's independence by Foreign Minister Rudolf Holsti.[39] The primacy of security policy in Finland's external policy is due to the inadequacy of existing security arrangements. The primacy of foreign policy in attaining security policy objectives and the degree of distinction that exists between foreign and defence policy indicates that Finns do not feel that their security can be adequately taken care of by military power alignments. It is thus that the consciousness of a dilemma in a crisis-conflict situation spurs on Finnish foreign policy in its search to find peaceful solutions and structures of international cooperation; to be, in short, eirenistic in its goals. This is the motivation that brought the Finns to take part in peacekeeping, mainly in Cyprus and Suez; to host part of the SALT talks—and to provide their own scheme for the creation of a non-nuclear zone in Northern Europe; to promote and in part host the European Security Conference; to put forward Jakobson for the post of UN Secretary-General.

These démarches, the significance of which some commentators tend to readily dismiss,[40] serve a double purpose. Through them the Finns are helping to promote the reduction in international tension which automatically works to the benefit of a vulnerable border-state like Finland. In addition, the Finns are able to build up, through démarches of this kind, a series of contact points and relations with the rest of the world that will tend, by their very existence, to make crises in their relations with the Soviet Union less likely to occur, either because the other contact points and relations form part of a network valuable to the Russians themselves or simply because the Soviet Union might be the recipient of negative reactions from these contacts if Finland began to be pressed by the Soviet authorities. The double aspect of this Finnish policy, the promotion of détente and the building up of international contact-points, serves first in a general way to prevent the emergence of a conflict situation that would cause the Finnish dilemma to materialize, and in the second place serves to prevent crises escalating in peacetime conditions from a too-zealous desire on the Soviet side to activate some aspects of the treaty negative to the Finns—say, military consultations.

The problem of Finlandization

With such a motivation, Finnish foreign policy cannot be regarded as being almost entirely subordinate to the Soviet Union—the doctrine of Finlandization, or *Finnlandisierung-Fernsteuerung*, to quote the formulation of one of the more prominent exponents of the belief, the Norwegian strategist Nils Ørvik. This doctrine sees a loss of autonomy in Finnish policy arising in part from goodwill, in part from blindness, and in part from the sycophancy engendered by the comforting fog of peaceful coexistence, but above all from an ever increasing pressure from the Soviet Union: it is Sovietization the soft way.

Those who believe in Finlandization see a country losing its independence in policy-making in two stages. In the first stage the country concerned, while retaining its traditional institutional forms, adapts both the personnel of its government and its decisions of external policy either to the dictates of the Soviet Union or to what it feels Russia really wishes. In the second stage the process of adaptation has gone so far as to divide or sap the energies of the nation, which then becomes unable to resist further pressures. Some pessimists already see Finland entering the second stage: for them the defeat of Jakobson's candidature for the post of UN Secretary-General confirmed the effectiveness of Soviet control (for it is the common assumption that it was the Soviet Union which vetoed Jakobson—a charge Russia has never bothered to refute) confirmed the effectiveness of Soviet control in the first stage of Finlandization —it was the last unsuccessful fling of Finnish foreign policy. Moreover, the perpetual presidency of the pro-Soviet Urho Kekkonen, re-elected for a fourth term in 1974 without having to face an opposition candidate, would seem to be ample testimony to Finland's sapped vitality.[41]

It may be said at once that the believers in Finlandization overlook the complexities both of the international political scene and of Finland's internal political, social, and economic life, where after a long struggle Kekkonen has come to embody an internal consensus that is equally important for Finland's relations with say, the EEC as it is for its relations with Russia. However, despite its crudities, the doctrine cannot be ignored for three reasons. The first of these is that the doctrine is a true one in the sense both of being a belief and of having, potentially, general applicability. For if such an optimistic analysis as Vital's can see Finland's adaptability to the Soviet Union as a 'paradigm for the future' which might have relevance to conflict areas of the world such as the Middle East or South East Asia, such a pessimistic politician as Franz-Josef Strauss sees instead a 'Finlandized' Finnish-Soviet relationship in a firm European perspective: it is the fate that awaits all states which remain unaware of the menace of creeping Sovietization. According to this viewpoint, all attempts to achieve détente with the Soviet Union (such as those contained in Willy Brandt's Ostpolitik) weaken the West Europeans' will and lead to a situation in which the Soviet Union, backed by overwhelming military strength, could then gradually pressure Western Europe to do its bidding.

It is, of course, hardly surprising that there is in many fields a clear correspondence between Finnish and Soviet foreign policy, though the scope of the former, as the policy of a small state, must necessarily be more restricted. Yet it must at once be noted that in recent years Finnish foreign policy-makers have shown themselves to be increasingly ambitious in regard to the role to be played by their country in Europe and the world. This increasingly active foreign policy, which is in total contrast to the passivity of Finnish foreign policy in the decade and a half after World War II, has been 'understood' in Western Europe and the United States—at least at the official level. The 'understanding' implies a recognition of a distinctive Finnish policy—distinctive in whatever degree—from that of the Soviet Union. For example, Jakobson's candidature for the post of UN Secretary-General was more than 'understood' in the West—it was approved and regarded as practicable. Again, Finland's promotion of the European Security Conference in 1969 was welcomed by the major West European powers: 'The Finnish approach to us made the whole concept more palatable', commented one Western diplomat. However, this might be dismissed as a product of joint Finnish-Soviet cooperation, as the sort of policy to be expected from a small state whose fortunes are so closely bound up with those of the Soviet Union—and indeed, the Soviet delegate to the Security Conference preliminaries is reported to have told the Swiss ambassador that the Soviet authorities certainly do seek to utilize Finland's mediatory role in relations with countries suspicious of Soviet intentions.

But those who persist in reading Finnish policy in the simplistic terms of its being a front for Soviet démarches fail to understand the policy of both countries. From the standpoint of Finnish policy, it may for example be argued that such an interpretation fails to appreciate the significance for Finland of Jakobson's candidature and also of the criticism of that candidature within Finland. From the standpoint of Soviet policy, opinion that sees Finnish policy as a front for the Soviet line overestimates the significance of Finland for the Soviet Union and overlooks the limited nature of the relationship.

In seeking to counter belief in creeping Sovietization, George Kennan has asked the adherents of this doctrine to re-examine their anxieties more from the standpoint of the problems of their own society and less from the point of view of their single-minded preoccupation with possible Soviet pressure, for Kennan believes that the Soviet Union is 'most unlikely to make specific demands on Europe under threat of force'.[42] Max Jakobson who, as diplomatist, historian, and apologist for his country cannot in any sense be regarded as truckling to the Soviet viewpoint, has expressed a similar opinion in regard to the Soviet attitude to Northern Europe.[43] Kennan himself bases his optimism on a fundamental belief that the power-potential of Western Europe and its US ally is anyway great and could be greater still if Soviet pressure were exerted. Aside from Kennan's argument, we may note that as far as the Finnish leaders are concerned, they will not commit themselves on Western Europe's power-potential, but in the exercise of their foreign policy they none the less assume the maintenance of a strong Western position, and the objective of their foreign policy is to accord with and utilize both West and East. Finland's present policy therefore cannot be a negative model for a future decline of Western Europe, for it assumes for its operation a strong Western Europe.

Once this is understood, the idea of Finlandization *as a doctrine of general applicability* loses validity. Similarly, once Finland's policy is seen as a whole, and Finland's successful attempts to maintain and strengthen its relations with the West are recognized, the concept of Finlandization will be found to be a woefully inadequate summary of Finnish policy too. But however inadequate it may be, the concept of Finlandization has nevertheless arisen and the second reason why this concept cannot be ignored is because it does represent an attempt to understand the situation of Finland in Europe, and in particular to understand the complex Finnish-Soviet relationship.

Ever since the president of Finland, Urho Kekkonen, said in a speech of 19 November 1961 at the height of the 1961 'note crisis' already described that the visit to Norway of the West German defence minister, Franz-Josef Strauss, was 'an incredible disservice to us', the idea of Finlandization has slowly gathered strength, seeping out of the studies of academics to blur the image of Finnish foreign policy.[44] The growing use of this concept particularly by German and Austrian commentators, at the end of the 1960s, remained unheeded by the Finns. For this was the period when they could look with pride on the increasing achievements of an active foreign policy, and to Finnish decision-makers such a policy meant by implication not pressure from behind but freedom from pressure—in contrast to the preceding decade when Finland dared say very little for fear of upsetting the Soviet Union. By the early 1970s, however, the Finnish government was compelled to note the occasional and unfortunate uses of this term by certain Western diplomats. This was doubly irritating and paradoxical to the Finnish leaders because in fact they had been struggling for years to convince their own nation that Finland had not become the victim of a soft form of Sovietization but was able to pursue an independent policy. We are therefore immediately brought up against another reason why the concept of Finlandization cannot be overlooked entirely. For those who believe that it is a reality can find evidence for their viewpoint not merely in Finland's internal political life, but also from people active in that life, from the dissidents of the Finnish political scene, like the Rightist Tuure Junnila, who have refused to be persuaded that Finnish foreign policy was necessarily running in the most favourable direction. It may, of course, be argued that this evidence is partisan and comes from those who, by virtue of social and political changes in Finland, are becoming more and more excluded from decision-making there. The fact remains that there is a challenge, however weak, from within Finnish society and that there exists a level of dissatisfaction —with some aspects at least of Finnish-Soviet relations—that affects a much wider group of Finns than might at first seem apparent; people, in short, who might regard postwar Finnish foreign policy as on the whole careful and constructive. It was not, for example, only the extreme Right in Finland which became upset when a leading Finnish publishing house 'censored itself' from publishing *The Gulag Archipelago*. (The book is, however, being sold in Finland and in a Finnish version, though published in Sweden.)

Indeed the main burden of Finlandization seems to be felt internally. Thus the state-controlled radio and TV network tends to give prominence to unfavourable aspects of United States policy and to refrain from unfavourable comment on East European or Soviet affairs. Since the Soviet-Finnish declaration of 6 April 1973 included a statement that the mass media should refrain from harming the friendly relations between Finland and the Soviet Union, it would seem clear that this one-sided presentation by the mass media is in part at least imposed by the requirements of Finnish foreign policy, a negative consequence of the success of that policy. On the other hand, it has to be said that many political elements in Finland do not feel the force of any limitation upon internal expression. There is a growing Leftist mood in Finland that is both genuine and naïve and for those who share this mood it often appears that—in the 70s at any rate—it has been the United States rather than the Soviet Union that has infringed on the rights of small states in the world.

However, whatever may be said about the internal climate of opinion in Finland, it will be salutary to bear in mind that as far as Finnish foreign policy is concerned the general picture is a positive one, both for the Western states as well as for the Soviet Union.

In speaking of foreign policy Kekkonen himself has tried to put Finlandization within a broad, positive context and in a speech of 16 October 1974 he described it as simply a means of explaining reconciliation with the Soviet Union, while those who used this term derogatorily, he implied, were really opposed to reconciliation with the Soviet Union. But in an earlier interview in *Newsweek*, published on 3 September 1973, Kekkonen had taken a somewhat different line. Just as Kennan was to do a few months later, Kekkonen then stressed Finland's special circumstances; so much so that the whole interview appeared in the light of the catch-phrase 'Finlandization is not for export'.

If the latter is really the case, we must descend from the euphoric level, referred to on p. 39, at which Finland is said to be serving as a pioneer in East-West relations—even showing the way to states more powerful than itself.

Friendship and cooperation

In looking at Finnish foreign policy we must bear the following points in mind. On the one hand, the existence of a certain amount of

Finlandization does not mean that Finnish foreign policy is simply subordinate to that of the Soviet Union. On the other hand, Finnish policy cannot be regarded either—in spite of the natural pursuit of Finnish objectives—as hostile to Russia. For it is the ability of the Finns to work with the détente that they themselves believe the Soviet Union has genuinely been promoting for many years that is the hallmark of the success of Finnish policy. It cannot be over-emphasized that the problems of the Finnish dilemma do not commit the Finns to the viewpoint that the Soviet Union is an aggressive state. On the contrary, in spite of the fact that Finland shares the ideology of the West European states, it often seems from the Finnish point of view that the dangerous moves in Europe and elsewhere are made by the West, and that it is these moves that then activate the Soviet Union. This is how, more and more, the Finns read the recent decades of European history.

Since foreign policy bears the main burden of Finnish security policy, and since the Finns' fundamental security problem lies in their handling of their relations with the Soviet Union, it is natural that they should endeavour to maintain and extend friendly relations with Russia. It is in this sense that the 1948 Treaty is the corner-stone of foreign policy, for the treaty provides the foundations of good relations between the two states in peacetime, even though, historically speaking, it took time for goodwill between the two states to develop on its basis.

Just as the treaty bears with it the danger that the 'friend' will turn out to be the 'enemy' in a crisis-conflict situation, so in peace-time circumstances at any rate it transforms the 'enemy'—who in 1941 was called the 'hereditary enemy' by President Ryti—into the 'friend'. On the basis of the friendship made explicit by the treaty, the sixth article of the treaty would seem to follow naturally. This reads: 'The High Contracting Parties pledge themselves to observe the principle of mutual respect of sovereignty and integrity and that of non-interference in the internal affairs of the other state'.

These words have a somewhat hollow sound for those who, whether in Finland or outside, believe in Finlandization as a reality. Indeed there is ample evidence from postwar Finnish history that the Soviet Union's expressed dislike of certain Finnish politicians and preference for others has had its effect on Finland's internal political life. But in a broader sense the treaty does serve to preserve Finland's constitutional, political, and social life. Under normal conditions, as long as the Finnish government and people feel able to adhere to the stipulations of the treaty and can communicate this to the Soviet authorities, the latter have little need to precipitate the creation of a communist state in Finland. Understandably, therefore, there is a need felt by many shades of the political spectrum in Finland to demonstrate the importance of the treaty. It is significant that this is being increasingly done by emphasizing other aspects of the treaty than the provisions of the first two articles. In the celebrations held in 1973 to commemorate the 25th anniversary of the treaty Ulf Sundqvist, a Social Democratic minister, singled out for attention the opportunities for cultural and economic cooperation with the Soviet Union afforded by Article 5. No minister (of whatever party) and no official (of whatever political affiliations and sympathies) would be inclined to underestimate the importance of the military-political articles of the treaty. At the same time it may not be without significance that a Foreign Office official publicly declared earlier in 1973 that the point of emphasis in the treaty had moved from the first two articles to friendship and cooperation in non-military matters.[45]

The Soviet dilemma

Since the setting up of the Soviet state, the security problem created by the existence on its Western frontier of bourgeois border-states has been of enormous significance. These states were either unwilling, or where willing unable, to stem the eastward advance of Germany. Thus, in spite of initial Soviet disavowals of annexationist intent, crisis and opportunity have led the Soviet Union either to annex some of these states, as in the case of Estonia, Latvia, and Lithuania, or to incorporate parts of other states, as in the case of certain areas of Germany, Poland, Czechoslovakia, and Romania, or instead, as in the case of the rest of Eastern Europe and half of Germany, to establish conditions for the creation of Socialist states, which *per se*, by virtue of their transformed economic and social system, would be friendly to the Soviet Union.

Finland was not transformed in this way, but did suffer territorial loss after the Winter War and the Continuation War. Roughly one-eighth of the country was ceded to the Soviet Union, including on both occasions Finland's second largest city of Viipuri and on the second occasion the port and province of Petsamo on the Arctic coast. Both in 1940 and in 1944 a large part of the province of Karelia was lost to Finland and the frontier was moved back from a distance of only 30 kilometres from Leningrad to a new line drawn approximately 180 kilometres from the former Russian capital.

Nevertheless Finland retained an exceptional position by comparison with the other border states. The only parallel is, to some extent, with Austria. Austria, indeed, did not lose any territory as a result of the war but was in fact re-born, its re-birth being a part of a dismemberment of Germany. Since, however, Austria, like Finland, had been involved on the German side in World War II, it was an understandable feature of Soviet postwar policy to ensure that both states should remain restricted in their military potential, an objective attained as far as Finland was concerned by the limitations on its armed forces in the peace treaty, while similar restrictions on the equipment of the Austrian armed forces were written into the second part of the Austrian State Treaty of 1955. And there are other points of comparison from the Soviet standpoint in the postwar position of these two states. The willing adoption by the Austrians of neutrality in their Neutrality Law passed on 5 November 1955 and communicated to foreign governments on 14 November was some guarantee to the Soviet Union that Austria would not enter into any military or political alignment against Russia.[46] As far as the Finns were concerned, the Soviet Union had this guarantee in another form, for Article 4 of the 1948 Treaty, confirming Article 3 of the 1947 peace treaty (which in turn confirmed Article 3 of the peace treaty that concluded the Winter War), states that 'The High Contracting Parties confirm their pledge . . . not to conclude any alliance or join any coalition directed against the other High Contracting Party'. Thus far, therefore, Austria and Finland are to be kept by the Soviet Union as weak states, their capacity for action circumscribed, whether internationally as in the case of the Austrian State Treaty, or more bilaterally as in the case of the two Finnish treaties.

But here the comparison between Austria and Finland must end, for as far as Finland is concerned, its weak position can be transformed in one particular: a strengthening element can be injected on the basis of the Finnish-Soviet military-political relationship enunciated in the first two articles of the 1948 Treaty. (Just as through similar treaties the Soviet Union can also stiffen the East European states that were formerly allies of Germany—Romania, Bulgaria, and Hungary.) Austria has nothing comparable to this. Significantly the Soviet Union has not acceded to an Austrian request to be able to furnish their armed forces with guided missiles, whereas the Finns, as we have seen, got these in 1962. In spite of the fact that the Austrians have quoted the Finnish case as a precedent, the Russians have not yielded. In this light the employment in Austria of the term '*Finnlandisierung*' to cast doubts on the neutrality that the Finns claim, and by implication to illumine the more pristine case of neutrality that the Austrian position represents, may be seen to be motivated in part by a jealousy of the positive aspects for Finland of the Finnish-Soviet bilateral relationship, a matter that will be touched on further in chapter 3.

It still remains that the Soviet attitude to Finland is an ambivalent one. On the one hand Finland must apparently continue to be in a weak position—the present armaments should suffice, as the Soviet ambassador said in April 1968.[47] On the other hand Finland must be strong enough to fulfil its obligations to the Soviet Union—train tough soldiers, as Marshal A. A. Grechko advised on a visit to Finland in 1971—and may even increase its troops in a conflict situation, as the commander-in-chief of the Warsaw Pact forces, Marshal Yakubovsky, is reported to have said some years ago.

This ambivalence shows that the Soviet Union has a problem of trusting Finland. But the paradox is that the Soviet-Finnish relationship is ultimately based on trust. Where there is no trust and a crisis-conflict situation occurs, Russia must use other means that will destroy the duality of the relationship and possibly the country's independence. It is in this sense that the younger Leftist critics in Finland, who are gaining an increasing say in devising their country's external policy, turn the Finnish dilemma, as sketched out a few pages earlier, on its head and argue that only by showing a prior willingness to cooperate fully with the Soviet Union in a crisis-conflict situation can Finland's integrity be maintained. Trust will, apparently, lead to trust.

The Soviet Union must be assured of a Finnish government that will adhere to the 1948 Treaty.[48] But Finland is a pluralistic, bourgeois society, with varying shades of opinion and possible coalitions between political-interest groups. The tool of analysis used by the Russians to measure the nature of bourgeois society, namely a study of 'the alignment of forces' in it, shows that this alignment is fluid and that, for example, anti-Soviet forces can influence and convert forces hitherto friendly to the Soviet government. The Russians therefore seek to find sure allies within the bourgeois groups that control a bourgeois society—and these allies must continue to demonstrate their reliability by protestations of understanding of Soviet security interests, which, in the Finnish case, means above all else praise of the 1948 Treaty—and appreciation of any dangers the Soviet Union may see looming up from Western Europe.

Inevitably, therefore, in spite of what is written in Article 6 of the 1948 Treaty on 'non-interference in the internal affairs of the other state', the Soviet Union has a distinct interest in Finland's internal politics and can exhibit clear preferences and dislikes, which the Finnish electorate becomes aware of.

Moreover, despite the development of relations of peaceful coexistence between Finland and the Soviet Union, the latter has not abandoned its special relationship with the country's Communist Party and SKDL front. This is because peaceful coexistence itself is a 'form of historic contest on a global scale between capitalism and socialism', which favours, according to the CPSU's leading theoretician, Mikhail Suslov, 'the further advance of the revolutionary forces',[49] with which the Soviet Union identifies.

In recent years one Soviet ambassador, Alexei Belyakov, is said to have overstepped the line of diplomatic proprieties and entered into discussions with the Stalinist (in a Finnish context this means more orthodox) wing of the Finnish Communist Party, a matter that came swiftly to the attention of the Finnish security police. In consequence of the disquiet shown from the Finnish side—the Finnish president is said to have expressed a clear distaste for the ambassador's clandestine meetings with the hardline Stalinists—the ambassador did not return to his post after a visit to his homeland.

This kind of incident (of a kind the existence of which is even stoutly denied by the more sceptical of Finnish writers on Finnish-Soviet relations)[50] should not blind us to the fact that in cultivating contacts with the Finnish Communist Party the Soviet Union is not expecting to rely on the Communist Party as its principal bulwark in the present Finnish system. Indeed, there is some evidence that in the last few years the Soviet government has not expected the Finnish Communist Party to take part in the government[51]—in this way the Communists can avoid bearing responsibility for any worsening in the position of the working class in an inflationary situation. The Finnish Communist Party itself, which participated in Popular Front governments from 1966 to 1971, has its own differences of opinion about this question, the Stalinist wing in particular asserting that participation in the government would weaken the fundamental Communist line. On the other hand, in a speech reported on the Finnish TV on 16 November 1974, the chairman of the party, Aarne Saarinen, urged all Left and Centre forces to unite for the next election. The Soviet Communist Party has continued to try to play the role of mediator between the two factions of the Finnish Communist Party—in February 1975 Finnish Communist leaders travelled to the Soviet Union for consultations that might help to resolve their differences. Since the Soviet Communist Party seems to lean towards the minority Stalinist wing of the Finnish party, the attempt at mediation secures little more than the maintenance of the superficial unity of the Finnish party that might otherwise split into two parties. Increasing Soviet press attacks upon Ele Alenius, the non-Communist chairman of the SKDL front, in which the Finnish Communist Party forms the core, hardly help the chances of the Finnish Communists to enter the government. Social Democratic leaders stated on 1 May 1975 that there was no immediate hope of cooperation with the Finnish Communists.

As far as the Soviet attitude to the internal political system in Finland is concerned, it does happen that the Russians' search for allies in the existing power-alignment and their concern to protect the Finnish Communist Party's interests coincide to some extent. Hence, in spite of the fact that the Social Democratic Party—which has given Finland most of its prime ministers since 1966—is now friendly to the Soviet Union in foreign policy outlook (a matter that was far from clear before the middle 60s), the Soviet Union itself may still prefer a Centre Party president to one from the ranks of the Social Democratic Party, for a president of Social Democratic origins who works well with the Soviet Union could enable the Social Democratic Party to steal the thunder of the Communists among the urban and working-class electorate—something the Centre Party cannot do. It is not without significance that the Centre Party took pride in receiving a delegation from the Soviet Communist Party in November 1974. However, it was the Finnish Social Democratic Party that took the initiative to solve this particular problem by openly proclaiming in April 1975 that they would sponsor the re-election in 1978 of President Kekkonen.

Much more important than all this, however, is the fact that once the Soviet Union has found allies within the existing, untransformed Finnish political system and in this way has become convinced that its security interests will be safeguarded, the basic Finnish-Soviet relationship can be expanded to Finland's benefit, and this can take place as a direct function of Soviet policy also. Addressing a meeting of the Finnish Foreign Policy Association on 22 April 1974, a Soviet diplomat, M. N. Streltsov, emphasized that Finnish-Soviet cooperation was increasingly taking place in ways that were significant internationally. He mentioned the agreement on economic, technological, and industrial cooperation concluded between Finland and the Soviet Union on 23 December 1971 and which had become 'a model for relations between lands with different social systems, as, for example, between the Soviet Union and France and between Poland and Sweden'. This innocent example illustrates the broader features of Finnish-Soviet cooperation that are serving to promote the spread of multilateral relationships in Europe, itself an essential objective of Finland's *security* as well as commercial policy.

In consequence it may be argued that the Soviet interest in the internal Finnish political system, an interest that is pre-eminently a search for allies within the system who believe in it, does not merely, as we have earlier argued, preserve the system, but also strengthens it—on the international plane. On the other hand this positive Finnish-Soviet cooperation in foreign policy may in turn demand so close a retention of the existing internal Finnish political system that the system becomes preserved in a stultifying and even atrophying manner. This is very relevant to the problem of the Finnish presidency.

So successful has President Kekkonen—president since 1956 and born 1900—been in developing and exploiting Finnish-Soviet relations that it has seemed both from the Finnish and Soviet side difficult to envisage a successor to him. After a short period of dis-avowing any intention of wanting to run for president last time, Kekkonen was persuaded to become president once more by the simple astonishing expedient of doing without a popular election and electing him by parliamentary vote. Thus while a bourgeois states-man, in the person of Kekkonen himself, continues to watch over the system, the system itself seems to have undergone a significant change from within, for the people, apparently, have lost a part of their rights and not too many voices were heard in opposition to this change, either, though the chairman of the Finnish-Soviet Friend-ship Society, Göran von Bonsdorff, did protest and ultimately resigned from his chairmanship.

The president is normally elected by the people (the year 1974 was an exception). Presidential power represents in certain matters a considerable modification of the parliamentary system; particularly is this so in the field of foreign policy-making where the president's role is of great importance and where his power has sometimes been exercised—as in the late 40s—in the face of parliamentary misgivings.

But it would be wrong to jump to hasty conclusions. When Kekkonen was re-elected by a parliamentary vote, a Constitutional Revisory Commission was then sitting and the initial mood of the Social Democratic members of that Commission had been to favour a change in the constitution that would make the presidency more dependent on parliament. In the event, because of conflicting viewpoints between the parties, no significant changes in the constitution are to be made. Most party opinion now considers that a strong presidency retaining direction of the country's foreign policy is essential, a viewpoint that also suits the Soviet position.

In the meantime Kekkonen himself has agreed to stand for re-election by the traditional means in 1978, i.e. by a popular election of an electoral college of 300 members, who will then elect the president. Since all the major parties, within and without the government, intend to support his candidature, however, no significant electoral contest will take place.

The Kekkonen candidature and his continuance in office should therefore be seen in the first place as a natural product of the consensus in foreign policy thinking that affects nearly all Finnish political parties nowadays. This consensus springs from a realization that the Finnish political forces that have shown a genuine friendship for the Soviet Union have been best able to protect Finland's own society and the specific interests of that society.

Because there is a Soviet dilemma underlying Finnish-Soviet relations, a dilemma of trust that the Soviet authorities always have when dealing with a capitalist society, it is inevitable that the Soviet Union makes clear its own preferences in Finnish presidential elections, as it did most determinedly in 1961 and 1968. On the other hand its preferences often coincide with those of the majority of the Finnish electorate, for whom a certain degree of radicalism in political life (and Kekkonen is a candidate of Finnish radicalism) is essential.

For many members of the younger generation in Finland this radicalism often takes the form of wanting to show themselves friendlier to the Soviet Union than their elders were, and on these grounds the Librarian of the Turku Municipal Library dithered about whether the library could lend out Swedish copies of *The Gulag Archipelago*, for 'there is a Soviet consulate in the town and relations between Turku and Leningrad are exceptionally good'.[52]

These incidents do not mean that Finnish society feels itself to be under pressure from the Soviet Union to transform itself as a whole. Under the leadership of those who have directed Finnish foreign policy in recent decades, Finland's links with Northern and Western Europe have strengthened. This is fundamentally an economic strengthening, as will be revealed in chapter 4. For the present we must note that Finland joined the UN and the Nordic Council in 1955, entered into a FINEFTA relationship with EFTA in 1961, joined the OECD in 1969, and signed a free-trade agreement with EEC in 1973. Such a society is not being Sovietized. Indeed, as one of the younger Social Democratic foreign policy critics (now himself involved in the conduct of his country's foreign policy) said to the author some years ago: 'In terms of defending their own society, which is a capitalist society, the leaders of Finnish foreign policy have done a very successful job'.

Notes

1. Jorma Kalela, *J. K. Paasikivi ja YYA-sopimus*, paper delivered to the Paasikivi Society in Helsinki, autumn 1970. For a contrary view of the influence of this group, see K. Brodin, 'Quo vadis, Finlandia'?, *Internationella studier* (Stockholm), 4 (1973).
2. K. Skyttä, *Presidentin muotokuva* (Helsinki, 1969), i. 279.
3. A view heartily echoed by the Soviet Union. See J. Komissarov, *Suomi löytää linjansa* (Helsinki, 1974), pp. 161 and 232.
4. M. Jakobson, *Finnish neutrality* (London, 1968), p. 54.
5. W. Churchill, *History of the Second World War* (London, 1948–54), v. 304–10.
6. O. Apunen, *Kansallinen realismi ja puolueettomuus Suomen ulkopoliittisina valintoina* (Tampere, 1972), i. 194.
7. Komissarov, pp. 154–5, quoting J. Blomberg and P. Joenniemi, *Kaksiteräinen miekka* (Helsinki, 1971), with approval. There is a strong similarity also between Komissarov's view and the view expressed in Apunen, p. 195.
8. Söderhjelm, pp. 166–7; L. Hyvämäki, 'Yhdysvallat ja YYA', *Kanava* (Helsinki), 7 (1974), pp. 391–8.
9. R. Ahtokari, *Asekätkentäjuttu* (Porvoo-Helsinki, 1971), pp. 153–4. Pohlebkin, p. 329, assumes his guilt.
10. Skyttä, i. 221; Ahtokari, pp. 77 and 94–5.
11. Pekka Peitsi (U. Kekkonen), *Tässä sitä ollaan* (Helsinki, 1944 ed.), pp. 63–80.
12. Skyttä, i. 249.
13. On the acceptance of Pekkala by the bourgeois forces, incl. Paasikivi, see Heikkilä, pp. 205–8.
14. L. Hyvämäki, *Vaaran vuodet* (Helsinki, 1957), p. 107.
15. A. Hautala, interviewed in *Ydin* (Helsinki), 2 (1974), p. 6.
16. M. D. Shulman, *Stalin's foreign policy reappraised* (Cambridge, Mass., 1963), p. 16.
17. *New Times* (Moscow), 13 and 45 (1949).
18. Ibid., 4 (1950).

19. J. Galtung, *The European Community* (London, 1973), p. 34.
20. *New Times*, editorial, 29 Mar 1950.
21. Ibid., 13 (1951).
22. Ibid., 25 (1951).
23. Ibid., 40 (1948) and 29 Mar 1950.
24. Ibid., 6 (1952).
25. E. Skog, *Sosialisti ja patriooti muistelee* (Porvoo-Helsinki, 1971), pp. 316–31.
26. *New Times*, 45 (1955). The article was entitled 'Finland and the Northern Council'.
27. *Int. Affairs* (Moscow), Jan 1968.
28. D. Vital, *The survival of small states* (London, 1971), ch. 4.
29. *Cooperation and Conflict*, 2 (1966).
30. Ibid.
31. N. M. Udgaard, 'Norway between East and West in World War II', ibid., 2 (1973), pp. 97, 99, and 103.
32. J. Nevakivi has written an important article on the British attitude to the 1944 armistice agreement in the *Helsingin Sanomat*, 15 Sept 1974.
33. Blomberg & Joenniemi, pp. 35 and 61 and chs 9 and 10.
34. Sihvo's viewpoints were expressed in a memorandum to President J. K. Paasikivi written in February 1947. It will be found in K. Lehmus, *Kolme kriisiä* (Helsinki, 1971), pp. 254–8.
35. See the interesting viewpoint put forward by K. Wahlbäck, 'Finnish foreign policy: some comparative perspectives', *Cooperation and Conflict*, 4 (1969), p. 290.
36. K. Brodin, *Finlands utrikespolitiska doktrin* (Stockholm, 1971), pp. 37–8.
37. N. Ørvik, *Sicherheit auf finnisch* (Stuttgart, 1972), p. 55.
38. A. Pajunen, 'Finnish security policy', *Cooperation and Conflict* (1968), p. 75.
39. K. J. Holsti, *Suomen ulkopolitiikka suuntaansa etsimässä vuosina 1918–22* (Helsinki, 1963), p. 65.
40. Ørvik, pp. 85 and 181–2.
41. Ørvik, pp. 136–40, connects Kekkonen's continuance with Jakobson's failure.
42. G. F. Kennan, 'Europe's problems, Europe's choices', *Foreign Policy* (New York), 14 (1974).
43. Jakobson, *Finnish neutrality*, pp. 92–4.
44. J-M Lafond, in his doctoral dissertation *Finlandisation* (Dijon, 1974), p. 6, finds the earliest reference to the idea of *Finnlandisierung* in K. Gruber's *Zwischen Befreiung und Freiheit* (Vienna, 1953), but in dealing with Finnish foreign policy on p. 252 Gruber does not actually use the term *Finnlandisierung*, which seems to have first been used several years later by Professor Richard Loewenthal. K. Korhonen's statement in *UPLA*, 1971, p. 30, on the origins of the term contains certain inaccuracies.
45. Korhonen, *Suomi toisen maailmansodan jälkeen*, p. 19.
46. B. Broms, *Itävallan pysyvän puolueettomuuden kehitys ja jäsenyys Yhdistyneissä Kansakunnissa* (Turku, 1968), pp. 54–74.
47. Wahlbäck, p. 296, quoting *Hufvudstadsbladet*, 7 Apr 1968.
48. For a recent Soviet opinion on these lines, see Komissarov, pp. 184–5.
49. Discussion in *The Times*, 3 and 4 July 1974, between E. M. Chossudovsky and R. Davy.
50. A. Tuominen, *Myrskyn mentyä* (Helsinki, 1971), pp. 79–81.
51. These viewpoints emerged in the spring of 1971 when the Soviet Union expressed fears of the softening of the Finnish Communist Party through its participation in the government (*Uusi Suomi*, 2 Apr 1971 and *Turun Sanomat*, 14 Apr 1971). Also J. H. Hodgson, 'Finnish communism and electoral politics', *Problems of Communism* (Washington), Jan–Feb 1974.
52. *Helsingin Sanomat*, 3 May 1974.

3 THE THEORY AND PRACTICE OF NEUTRALITY

So far Finnish neutrality has been referred to only incidentally in this work. It has been noted as an aspiration that emerged in 1918 in the first few weeks of the newly independent Finnish state, only to be rapidly replaced by a close relationship with Germany. In the 1920s and especially in the 1930s the concept of Finland as a neutral state strengthened, but was then shattered by the Winter War, the subsequent opposition of the Russians to Finland's participation in a Nordic Defence Alliance, and by the Finns' own alignment with Germany. Neutrality as a term descriptive of Finland's position between East and West gradually came into use once more in the post-World War II world. Here the Finns placed emphasis upon the phrase in the preamble to the 1948 Treaty with the Soviet Union that expressed the Finnish desire 'to remain outside the conflicting interests of the Great Powers'. If this is a definition of neutrality, it would seem, at first glance, to fit in badly with the first two articles of the treaty itself, which enjoin the conditions for military cooperation with the Soviet Union.

Leaving this problem for a moment, we can best approach an understanding of Finnish neutrality by seeing the idea in action. This draws us back once more to the 'note crisis' of 1961.

According to Kekkonen's own account of the settlement of the 'note crisis', it was not only the simple fact of trust in the Finnish leadership that was instrumental in persuading the Soviet authorities to withdraw their demand for military consultations. The Finns had also something specific to point out to the Soviet Union. At Novosibirsk Kekkonen told Khrushchev that if consultations occurred, the danger of 'war psychosis' might grow in Scandinavia. This would mean greater military preparations in Norway and Denmark—and also in Sweden. In this period the Norwegian and Danish politicians were actually informing their fellow countrymen and the rest of the world that they were not going to be browbeaten by the Soviet Union and that, if necessary, they would review their whole policy of only having a limited commitment to NATO and go the whole way.[1] The Soviet leaders were thus compelled to accept what had so far happened in the North (e.g. the creation of the unified Baltic command) for fear that if they did not, further military developments there would distort the Northern Balance still more. It appears that the Soviet authorities had to cut their losses.

On the other hand the fact is that from the Soviet point of view the manipulation of the Northern Balance has a limited function. If the Northern Balance is disturbed from Norway and Denmark, the real point of Soviet compensatory policy might be to increase, say, the potential of the Murmansk base area, which indeed occurred in the 1960s. Finland is not really the point of a genuine military compensation, though as a *political* move the Soviet Union might seek to activate the treaty. Still the true purpose of Soviet policy towards the whole of Northern Europe once the Balance begins to swing is to stop the swing, even if this means accepting a more lop-sided balance once the position of rest is attained. All this Kekkonen divined. It is in the Soviet interest to keep Norway and Denmark as contented as possible in their not-quite total commitment to NATO, failing the attempt to persuade them to leave NATO. Similarly Sweden must stay neutral, and suspicions that Sweden was defaulting on its neutrality were expressed in the Soviet note to Finland. But Sweden should not be driven, by fear of Soviet policy in regard to Finland, any further into NATO's arms.

Thus though the Soviet leaders started by reminding Finland, as they had reminded it over the past four years, of the German danger and the requirements of the 1948 Treaty, they ended the 'note crisis' by coming round to the Finnish position: that the less the treaty had to be implemented the happier the situation would be[2]— over the whole of Northern Europe, too. This was a boost for Finnish neutrality, for military consultations with the Soviet Union in peacetime would conversely have reflected negatively on that neutrality. Now it appeared that Finnish neutrality was a stabilizing factor in the North. The more the Finns reflected about their handling of the 'note crisis' the more exuberant they became, and by the end of the 1960s they were arguing that *they* had now the initiative in deciding whether or not to call for consultations under Article 2 of the treaty, an erroneous viewpoint that the Russians soon corrected.[3]

Once the flurry of the 'note crisis' subsided, Kekkonen himself was found to have gained enormously in prestige by his handling of the Soviet Union. His foreign policy line, of exerting effort to keep the trust of the Soviet authorities, appeared to have succeeded beyond all expectations. Not merely were the Soviet leaders again contented with Finland, but Finland seemed in connection with its increasingly-recognized neutrality to be able to pursue an active foreign policy of its own that had no clear reference at all to Soviet policy. Instead of being despised for his partiality to the Soviet Union, which had seemed to bring Soviet influence into internal Finnish political life, Kekkonen began to be appreciated for his ability to keep Soviet relations happy and the Soviet Union at a distance. By the middle of the 60s the Social Democratic Party as a whole adopted a new attitude towards the Soviet Union and since then the bulk, at least, of the Finnish Conservative Party has tried to follow suit. The latter have not succeeded as well as the former, who have not merely been in all governments since 1966, but have supplied most prime ministers since then, and even a foreign minister, in the person of Väinö Leskinen, who was a disciple of Tanner, but recanted to become *persona grata* to the Soviet government, thus demonstrating that the fluid nature of the alignment of forces in a bourgeois society can sometimes work or be made to work to the advantage of the Soviet Union.

In short, a growing consensus about foreign policy has been evident in Finland for the last decade. This is compounded of an absence of hostility to the Soviet Union and a trust that Finland can pursue its own line of policy. Positively this consensus comes to rest in neutrality, which every political party and stream of thought in Finland now accepts as the frame of Finnish foreign policy. It has not always been so. The Communists in the negotiations about the 1948 Treaty wanted no talk of neutrality from the Finnish side,[4] but the gradual acceptance by the Soviet Union of neutrality as the input into the Finnish-Soviet relationship from the Finnish partner has won them round. In addition, the strong position that Kekkonen has with the Soviet authorities has meant that the Communists in Finland have not since 1961 had a candidate of their own for president and have not wanted to speak in any way against the Kekkonen Line.

With good reason therefore, leading Finns have referred to neutrality as a way of life for Finland. It is a binding force that has great internal significance. For Kekkonen himself, a renowned faction-fighter and, some would say, opportunist in his earlier political career, the question of national unity has become of overwhelming importance.[5] Not merely is this a question of finding for himself the necessary amount of automatic support that enabled him to become president once more in 1974 without having to go through the tedium of an election campaign, but there is at stake also the question of having a broad popular backing for Finland's foreign political initiatives. Thus in Finland a successful foreign policy, exemplified in the doctrine of neutrality, binds the nation together. At the same time a united nation is one of the conditions for the successful pursuit of such a policy. The relationship between the two is tight. Here then is the *Willenskraft* in the Finnish nation that Ørvik did not find.

It cannot be argued that because opposition to Kekkonen has more and more come to be concentrated in dissident fringe political groups the bulk of Finnish political life has in consequence become spineless. The coalition governments that have been in office since 1966 have been strong governments, based nevertheless on a compromise of mutual interests, Kekkonen having himself expressed the viewpoints that a two-party system on the Anglo-Saxon model would not be suitable for Finland,[6] for it would be socially and politically divisive. It is anyway in the period of office of the coalition governments of recent years that some of the more remarkable moves in Finnish foreign policy have been made.

The Finnish Foreign Office itself has been only too pleased to receive popular backing for its efforts. One of the more remarkable features of Finnish foreign policy-making in the late 60s and early 70s has been the willingness of some of the leading decision-makers to go and explain to public bodies and associations the nature and aims of the policy pursued. When head of the Political Department, Risto Hyvärinen, and the then assistant head, Keijo Korhonen, often spoke to conferences, meetings of reserve officers, universities, adult education centre groups, etc. It should be pointed out that in Finland the Foreign Service recruits its personnel not only by means of a regular graduate intake—where political factors may also be taken into account—but in addition there is a recruitment of experts from outside, many of whom are academics, like Korhonen, and many of whom have a clear political affiliation, like him. These experts may enter the career structure, as Hyvärinen, a former officer and a doctor of political science, has done—he is at present Finnish ambassador in Belgrade, or they may serve for a temporary period, as Korhonen, now Professor of Political History in the University of

Helsinki, has served—still nevertheless keeping up a connection with the Foreign Office.

The system of having political nominees appointed to the Foreign Service—Korhonen with his Centre Party background and Jaakko Blomberg and Osmo Apunen from the Social Democratic Party, to mention only a few examples—has come in for some criticism in Finland. But it is a system that does connect the Foreign Service with representative currents of opinion in the country. Nor does the system of recruiting experts exclusively favour the party-card. Hyvärinen and Jakobson have no specific party affiliation, though Jakobson once worked as London correspondent of the Conservative newspaper *Uusi Suomi*.

In any case the rather heterogeneous background of some of the leading Foreign Office officials has undoubtedly helped to foster the popularization of foreign policy among many citizen-groups and shades of opinion in Finland. But popularization, in the sense of an active campaign to convince the Finnish people of the virtues and benefits of neutrality, has also a strong aspect of manipulation. For since Finnish foreign policy is active, and active neutrality has been the avowed character of the Kekkonen Line, there are goals served by neutrality over and above the value of the concept as a kind of internal cement. But what goals does neutrality serve? It is easy to lull the Finnish public with accounts of the prestige won for Finland by her sponsoring and part hosting of the European Security Conference or the part hosting of the SALT talks, but what is all this a part of?

Neutrality is not a simple concept, especially for a country whose status is as difficult to define as Finland's is. Assuming that neutrality can be reconciled with the 1948 Treaty, to what end is this being done? Part of the answer will be found in the next chapter, where economic questions will be discussed. Of pre-eminent importance in this matter, however, are the basic considerations of security policy which constitute the theme of this chapter. And when neutrality is looked at in terms of security policy it will be soon evident that the apparent consensus ruling on this matter only serves to hide a number of shifting and sometimes conflicting doctrines of what neutrality is for Finland. Behind the consensus even party politics may be seen to be operating.

As a starting-point the analysis of one of Finland's own commentators on security policy, Harto Hakovirta, should be noted. According to Hakovirta Finland did not attain what he calls 'symmetrical neutrality' until the years 1961–2.[7] This was the time when Kekkonen made his explanatory visits to Britain, Austria, and the United States (1961) and France (1962). At this point Finnish neutrality began to be accepted by the West as well as by the East. In this respect Finland's position was balanced between West and East. We must ask why the Finnish leaders desired such a balance.

A neutral borderland

Finland's 1948 Treaty with the Soviet Union is a defence treaty. It is also a treaty of friendship. These two aspects would seem to close out the possibility of an attack from the Soviet Union through or against Finland. If Russia ever felt the need to move forward through Finnish territory to prevent aggression from a German move in the North, it would do so presumably after consultations with and the permission of the Finns.

But the 1948 Treaty, the text of which has remained unaltered in subsequent renewals, reflected the Stalinist concept of a defence in depth of the Soviet Union. This soon began to be out of date with the growth, after the middle 50s especially, of Soviet military power and the changes in thinking of Soviet military experts according to which 'the offensive constitutes the basic method of warfare and orienting oneself on the strategic defensive . . . means dooming oneself beforehand to irreparable losses and defeat'.[8] In short, the question was of the pre-emptive strike. The revelations of the Czech political general Jan Šejna, who defected to the West in 1968, emphasized the fact that the Soviet Union in a conflict situation with the West intended to strike through Finland and aimed to get through in twenty-four hours. It was significant that his statement stung a Finnish officer to put pen to paper and assert that it would take the Soviet Union a lot longer than twenty-four hours to make the trip across Finland. The Finns were going to resist to some effect, apparently.[9]

The Finnish army's interest in and training for guerrilla warfare also points in the same direction. Military discussion papers entitled *Surprise Attack*[10] envisage the eventuality of Finnish urban centres under a foreign occupation with resistance, however, continuing in the Finnish hinterland of forests and fells—a very dubious scheme, taking into account the growing urbanization of Finland and the increasing chances therefore of holding the civilian population as hostages. These thoughts about contingency planning can hardly

concern a possible occupation by NATO forces—which might anyway well be made up of brother Scandinavians. No, this type of
contingency-thinking concerns a possible conflict with the Soviet
Union.

The fact is that the 1948 Treaty leaves a number of questions
unanswered in Finnish-Soviet relations and the Finnish army has,
as any army in this position must, to think therefore to some extent
of what it would do if a breakdown in these relations occurred,
however unlikely this contingency may seem. In submitting his
viewpoint to the Finnish Parliamentary Defence Committee, which
issued its report in 1971, Professor Jan-Magnus Jansson, the chairman of the Committee, admitted that a defence of Finnish neutrality
must take into account the theoretical possibility of a defence of this
neutrality against the Soviet Union, but then, added Jansson, 'our
foreign policy will have broken down'.[11] The definition of Finnish
security policy mentioned in chapter 2—namely that security policy
is an equation of foreign policy plus defence policy—may be worth
recalling here, for in this equation defence policy is accorded an
autonomous status.

The readiness to defend the country against aggression from any
quarter would seem to be required by historical precedent and
customary opinion for Finland to be regarded as a neutral state. At
first sight there is no conflict with the 1948 Treaty in this, for if
Finland received Soviet aid under the treaty 'Germany and its
allies' would already have infringed Finnish neutrality by an act of
aggression, so that the Soviet Union would turn out to be the
protectors of Finnish neutrality. On the other hand existing Finnish
security arrangements certainly seem to be of an un-symmetrical
nature. Who comes to Finland's aid if the Soviet Union attacks it—
as part, say, of a pre-emptive thrust through to the West? The
fourth article of the 1948 Treaty enjoins on both parties abstinence
from 'any alliance . . . or coalition directed against the other High
Contracting Party'. And thus although, as some Finnish experts
imply,[12] it would be still possible for Finland to have a defence
agreement with another power (possibly Sweden) against aggression
from another quarter (the Soviet Union), in fact it would be all too
easy for the Soviet leaders to label any such agreement as being
aggressive in turn to the Soviet Union. The best the Finns can hope
for therefore is a symmetrical recognition of Finnish neutrality by
both East and West.

There are some problems in achieving this. Finland is committed by the 1948 Treaty to a defence not merely of its own territory but also of the Soviet Union, if the latter is attacked through Finnish territory. This is a strange obligation for a neutral to undertake,[13] i.e. to defend under certain circumstances a great power, but alternatively this obligation does presuppose the strictest, most absolute form of neutrality—no transit agreements across Finnish territory such as the Swedes had with the Germans in World War II. Again, however, the holding of military consultations with the Soviet Union in peacetime if a threat of aggression from Germany or its allies is established (Article 2) casts its own shadow over Finnish neutrality.

In 1965 President Kekkonen expressed himself pessimistic about the chances of Finland remaining outside the conflagration if war occurred in Europe. In the 1968 presidential election campaign he was upbraided for this by his Conservative opponent Matti Virk-kunen, who insisted that Finland should aim to be neutral in war by building up a strong defence force of its own.[14] In spite of the bitter wrangling that then ensued between the two men, the difference of viewpoint between them was not one of principle but only of estimation of possibilities. For Kekkonen committed himself also to the line that if war broke out Finland's first declaration was to be one of neutrality (in the light of the preamble of the 1948 Treaty) and that it was to this aim that the peacetime policy of seeking recognition of neutrality was directed.[15] This is what Hyvärinen had said in 1965 and Kekkonen's foreign minister Ralf Törngren in 1959, and it was what the Parliamentary Defence Committee was to say in 1971.[16]

Why then was Kekkonen so pessimistic in 1965? His own explanation, given a few months later, was that he had been thinking primarily of Lapland. The fact was that, with the tremendous military build-up in the Soviet Murmansk area and the general growth of Soviet offensive capability, it was the northern part of Finland that was most vulnerable, whether from the point of view of a Soviet advance into Norway across Sweden and northern Finland or from the point of view of countermeasures from the NATO side. The strategic position in the rest of Finland had actually improved. This has even given rise to speculation in Finland that it would be wise therefore to give Lapland away and thus secure Finland's neutrality.[17]

Kekkonen is not a giver-away of territory and in spite of Lapland's poverty-stricken nature no political group in Finland would ever support the abandoning of the province. On the other hand a Soviet sweep through Lapland (in effect a transit agreement?) to forestall a NATO advance could leave the rest of Finland under the protection of its own army, with the country still proclaiming its neutrality. The neutrality would of course be benevolent to the Soviet Union, as Swedish neutrality was in practice benevolent to the Germans in World War II.

Speculations of this kind about Finland's security-political position hardly ever reach the surface in Finland. Indeed, as if to counter such *hidden* thoughts, the Finns moved a battalion of troops to Sodankylä in Lapland in 1965 in the hope of demonstrating to the Norwegians that Finland did intend to see that Lapland remained in Finnish hands.

What can be said is that at the heart of Finnish policy there exists a confusion as to what the position of neutrality in a conflict situation means for Finland. Hakovirta, in a work that is used as a course-book in Finnish universities, seems to argue in favour of an attempt to maintain neutrality in a threatening conflict situation.[18] Those who incline to the Right in their political outlook (and here must be included people without a party-card like Hyvärinen and Jakobson, or members of parties other than the Conservative Party like the Swedish People's Party ministers J-M Jansson and the 1974 minister of defence, Kristian Gestrin) believe strongly in the need to attempt a position of neutrality in war. For these representatives the 1948 Treaty refers to a 'special relationship with the Soviet Union built into [our] neutrality'.[19] For them, that is, neutrality takes precedence over the 1948 Treaty, which is subordinated to the needs of neutrality.

The other camp, whose clearest exponents are Blomberg and Joenniemi, consist of Leftist Social Democrats and SKDL, whose two representatives on the Parliamentary Defence Committee expressed a minority dissenting opinion. For this group the prime fact in a conflict situation is the strength of Finland's relationship with the Soviet Union as embodied in the 1948 Treaty. Neutrality takes its colour from this.

Centre Party attitudes are more difficult to define. Korhonen has been inclined to put out cautious views,[20] while the present foreign minister, Ahti Karjalainen, has expressed himself as being somewhat tired of the continual attempts made to define neutrality,[21] which he has likened to the debates of the medieval scholastics. According to a statement reported in the Communist *Kansan*

Uutiset on 28 January 1975, Karjalainen had committed himself to the viewpoint that the Finnish army had no decisive significance in a general war, a view the commander of the Finnish defence forces, General Lauri Sutela, seemed to question in an interview published in the Conservative *Uusi Suomi* on 11 March 1975. It was not without significance that in the meantime Pertti Joenniemi, in a TV discussion held on 13 February 1975, had extended Karjalainen's statement to mean that the Finns had now come to recognize that no problem of defending their country against a threat from the Soviet side existed. The key figure is, of course, the Finnish president. Experience has shown that he manipulates many ideas and persons: some of the ideas and persons fall, as Hyvärinen and Jakobson fell, while he remains, the continuing embodiment of his country's good relationship with the Soviet Union.

The Soviet point of view is no longer in doubt. As noted in the previous chapter, the mysterious figure of Yuri Komissarov has pronounced against an earlier opinion of a Soviet savant, an opinion much quoted by the Finns, that the 1948 Treaty was really a treaty defining Finnish neutrality and was not a military alliance. The guideline that Komissarov has taken is the argumentation of *Kaksiteräinen miekka*.

The differing views put forward in Finland as to what neutrality means in a conflict situation illustrate yet another aspect of the fundamental dilemma of Finnish security policy. The connection with earlier Finnish thinking on foreign policy should, however, be noted. There is a persistent tendency in Finnish foreign policy to want to solve the country's security problems without too close a reliance on a foreign power. Thus, in splendid disdain of the 1948 Treaty, Jakobson informed the Security Council, in a statement made on 24 January 1969, that Finland has not based its security 'on military alliances or the protection of any state or one group of Powers'. In the edited version of his talk the reference to 'any state' was deleted.[22]

Small wonder is it that there is a mood in Finland to want to evade these basic questions of security policy and to concentrate instead on measures of what the Finns call *neutrality policy*. It is here that a near-consensus is often achieved.

In these acts of neutrality policy the symmetrical neutrality attained by the early 60s is of great importance, for the measures proposed by Finland gain credibility from Finland's neutral status. Neutrality testifies to the autonomous nature of these acts of policy, acts which, in a period of détente, may sometimes be similar to those proposed by the Soviet Union.

The North European nuclear-free zone and the neutralization of Norway

Because Finland's security problem does not permit of a clear solution in power terms, there is a marked tendency in Finnish policy to put neutrality to work for the de-escalation of power. This, in its regional context, aids the basic Finnish wish to be outside conflicts. It also identifies Finnish neutrality with a 'peace-loving policy' that fits in well with the Soviet aspirations expressed among other things in concepts like 'peaceful coexistence'. Increasingly—and it is a usage adopted from the Soviet Union—Finnish policy refers to its 'peace-loving' nature.

As we have seen in chapter 1, the Finns had already in 1958, even before the 'night frost crisis' endorsed, in a Soviet-Finnish communiqué their support for the creation of a Central European nuclear-free zone (the 1957 Rapacki plan). Nevertheless when Khrushchev in a speech in Riga on 11 June 1959 proposed the idea of a Scandinavian and Baltic nuclear-free zone, the Finnish leadership did not respond, for in the same speech Khrushchev attacked the Tannerites, NATO, and German militarism, and at this point of time the Finnish government was still endeavouring to avoid associating itself with this type of Soviet approach, Finland's preoccupation during these years being, as we have seen, to establish the credibility of its neutrality. The U2 flight and the 'note crisis' were factors that compelled Finnish policy, however, to face up to the realities of great power politics in a manner that went far beyond the task of defining Finland's status by seeking confirmation of Finnish neutrality from all and sundry. The Swedish foreign minister Östen Unden's proposal of 16 February 1962 for a non-nuclear club was officially welcomed in Finland therefore, and precisely because it was a proposal emanating from a North European neutral, was doubly welcome to the Finns. Since U Thant in the spring of 1963 began to encourage the member states of the UN to work for the creation of nuclear-free zones all over the world and since the Mexicans were then actively promoting a Latin American nuclear-free zone, President Kekkonen became emboldened to propose on 28 May 1963 the creation of a North European nuclear-free zone, a proposal that, in view of the growing and diverse international interest in schemes of this kind, could not be put down to Soviet pressure, in spite of the similarity of Kekkonen's plan with the ideas Khrushchev put out in 1959.

Kekkonen's plan, mooted in the year of the Partial Test-Ban Treaty, repeated in his speech in Moscow on 24 February 1965 and in a speech given in Helsinki on 29 November 1965, was carried into the UN at the end of the 60s and thence into the Geneva Disarmament Conference.

In 1972 the Finns brought the matter up in the UN General Assembly and, a year later, in the early days of the Security Conference. Further, as a result of their persistence, a working group was set up in the Geneva Disarmament Conference in March 1975 to investigate possibilities for creating additional nuclear-free zones in the world. In April Keijo Korhonen was unanimously elected chairman of this working group.

Because Kekkonen in his 1965 speeches criticized West German participation in a multilateral nuclear force, and did so on the grounds that it would be regarded by the Soviet and other Warsaw Pact countries as a threat to peace, it is tempting to see the whole of Kekkonen's thinking about a Northern nuclear-free zone as being a reflection of the awareness of the danger of West German militarism, an awareness which the Soviet Union had finally succeeded in implanting in the Finns. But this would be far too simple an explanation. For the fact was that in launching the idea in 1963 Kekkonen had been thinking basically in global terms. It was the Cuban missile crisis of the previous autumn that he had, according to his own account, foremost in mind. Thus it was the United States and the Soviet Union as much as NATO and West Germany and the Soviet Union that Kekkonen was thinking of.

At first glance the plan for a North European nuclear-free zone appears to be of a somewhat superfluous nature. Finland cannot have nuclear weapons in the light of the stipulations of the 1947 peace treaty, Sweden will not have them, and Norway and Denmark will not have nuclear-bases on their soil in peacetime. In practice the Scandinavian area thus is a nuclear-free zone. All Kekkonen's proposal would achieve, so it seems, is to limit the political and military manœuverability of the three other Scandinavian states, who would henceforward not be able to use the threat of possessing or actual possession of nuclear-weapons as a last resort safeguard. Characteristic of Northern reactions was that of the Norwegian prime minister Einar Gerhardsen, who on 20 January 1964 mentioned that the plan might be considered if the Soviet Union would be prepared to join the plan at least as far as the Soviet areas bordering on Finland and Norway were concerned. From the point of view of military power, Kekkonen's plan so obviously favours the Soviet Union, whose nuclear potential at Murmansk remains untouched, at the expense of NATO.

The same might be said of another plan mooted by Kekkonen in 1965—his suggestion to neutralize the Norwegian-Finnish frontier which was mentioned again by the Finns in 1970. In Kekkonen's eyes the neutralization of this frontier would free Finnish Lapland from the threat of being contested for by the armies of the two blocs, for with Sweden neutral anyway and with Finland having a purely defence arrangement with the Soviet Union (the 1948 Treaty), all that is required is for a statement by the NATO side (i.e. Norway) that it does not harbour aggressive designs on this frontier. Once this is given, in the form of a neutralization of the Norwegian-Finnish frontier, Finland has reduced the vulnerability of its weakest area (Lapland), has reinforced its neutrality ('neutralization'), and has built up a kind of balanced security system, a balance between the 1948 Treaty and the Norwegian frontier neutralization that would indirectly bind NATO. Hence while in power terms it is impossible for the Finns to balance the 1948 Treaty, by thinking in terms of de-escalating power a certain balance in security can be achieved.

But the Norwegians have not seen matters in quite the same light. They have seen that their security depends in part upon the opportunity to escalate power, i.e. to receive nuclear weapons if necessary, and a frontier neutralization would impose a limitation on this possibility. Similarly the Norwegians have not taken kindly to a proposal first put out by the Finnish officer Aimo Pajunen in 1965[23] and referred to in Kekkonen's speech of 29 November of the same year, by which Norway should be encouraged to leave NATO and enter into an agreement with Britain and the United States on similar lines to the one between Finland and the Soviet Union embodied in the 1948 Treaty. In 1966 the Norwegian prime minister John Lyng pointed out to the Finns that the Northern Balance would tip dangerously for them if Norway did leave NATO.[24]

If Finland is seriously considering a defence of neutrality that also includes a defence of Finnish neutrality against possible Soviet aggression, the threat of which is the main problem for the Norwegians, then it is folly for the Finns to weaken NATO military potential in the North. Since, as remarked in the earlier pages of this chapter, there is reason to think that the Finnish military must at least give some consideration to the contingency of a Soviet attack, the conclusion to be reached is that there is a contradiction between an aspect of Finnish military policy and some of the démarches of the country's foreign policy. For if the Soviet Union did attack, it could not be in the interests of a resisting Finnish army to have NATO as far away as possible, which, apparently is what the foreign policy démarches of Finland described above are aiming at. It therefore looks as if Kekkonen, though he affirmed in 1968 that if war broke out Finland would first try to proclaim its neutrality, does not think much of the attempted military solution that this would imply. Here is the real basis of conflict with the rival presidential candidate, Matti Virkkunen, for Virkkunen, bearing in mind the desire to be neutral in war and the necessary defence of such a neutrality, wanted to increase the military budget. Kekkonen did not. This difference of opinion, which came embarrassingly to the surface in 1968, is generally smoothed over by statements to the effect that *foreign* policy is the main arm of security policy. The confusion that exists at the heart of Finnish security policy can nevertheless be illustrated by statements made by the defence minister, Kristian Gestrin, in the autumn of 1974: Gestrin pleaded for a stronger military presence in northern Finland and for the provision throughout Finland of a network of defence missiles, but when speaking of the Cyprus issue he committed himself to the general proposition that 'small states can in no situation build their security on arms'.

Is Finland then to rely for its security on a de-escalation of power in the North, and, as in the prewar world, on hopes that the whole Northern area will in consequence in some way remain outside the area of future conflict? How does this all tie up with the often expressed Finnish opinion that it is the nuclear balance of terror in the world that is the underlying element in the preservation of peace?[25] Are not the Finns effectively seeking to upset that balance by weakening NATO's presence in the North?

In seeking an answer to these questions, attention must be paid to an important opinion put out in Finland by the former Foreign Office official Osmo Apunen.[26] Apunen associates the Finnish proposal for a North European nuclear-free zone with Security Council resolution 255 (1968), which was passed in connection with the Non-Proliferation Treaty and was zealously promoted by Max Jakobson. This resolution provides for help for non-nuclear states under threat of attack. This help should come from the Security Council and in particular from the permanent members who have nuclear capacity themselves. As Apunen points out, there is a kind of guarantee here—and the most important guarantors are the United States and the Soviet Union.

In the meantime in October 1974 President N. Podgorny already assured the Finns that the Soviet leaders were prepared to guarantee a non-nuclear Northern Europe, which, as the *Helsingin Sanomat* pointed out in an editorial of 22 November 1974, was only a repetition of Khrushchev's earlier proposal. But the need for the Finns is for the West to respond. We may recall that one of the strongest Finnish impulses for promoting the original nuclear-free zone idea was consciousness of the global problem involved in the Cuban missile crisis, a problem of the possible nuclear conflict of the two superpowers who now, by a decision of the UN Security Council, are transformed into guardians of nuclear-free states. The theory of this has great appeal for Finnish policy-makers. It was Kekkonen himself who, reviewing his country's recent past in the course of a speech he made in Vaasa on 6 January 1967, said that 'we felt that neutrality, guaranteed by a *single* great power [my italics], was not a completely stable condition'.

While some Finnish experts, bearing in mind, for example, some of the objections expressed by the Norwegians to the plan for a North European nuclear-free zone, have suggested that the Soviet Union should now be asked to agree to the inclusion of certain of its border areas in the proposed zone,[27] Apunen himself remains wary of the idea. It does not seem to be the improbability of a Soviet response that disturbs Apunen. His caution seems rather to be motivated by thoughts about a guarantee by the two superpowers, which would hardly be possible if one (the Soviet Union) was actually a participant in the nuclear-free zone. In this connection we may note the importance for Finland of the SALT talks and their hosting in part from 1969 to 1972 in Helsinki. Nor have the Soviet authorities been at all disinclined to point out to the Finns the relevance of these talks to a nuclear-free Northern Europe. The link between the latter proposal and both SALT I (agreement on the numerical limitation on strategic missiles) and the continuing Moscow talks of June 1973, where both parties expressed their intention of working to achieve limitations on other aspects of nuclear armament, was brought out, if somewhat vaguely, by the APN correspondent L. Malov in an article in a Finnish Conservative newspaper in August 1974[28], at a time, that is, when Finnish spokesmen were again endeavouring to reactivate the North European nuclear-free zone plan.

The SALT talks do connect for the Finns with their widest hopes of seeing the two superpowers commit themselves to some form of guarantee, and this of course pre-eminently too in global terms. Superpower agreement on nuclear policy bears with it for the Finns the global guarantee that is the basis of the Finns' growing belief that they can come to think once again of security as essentially collective security. In thinking of the latter in 1944 Pekka Peitsi saw it as being inevitably based upon 'the open power politics' of the great powers.

While the US-Soviet axis is thus of fundamental importance for the Finns, the problem of NATO remains where, if the United States is the strongest power, the second strongest for the Finns and the Soviet Union is West Germany. The 1968 Non-Proliferation Treaty (NPT), which removed (at least temporarily) the fear of West German possession of nuclear-weapons was a positive factor for Finnish policy, bearing in mind persistent Soviet fears and the naming of Germany as the potential enemy in the 1948 Treaty. The NPT should reduce the dangers of West German military penetration of Northern Europe, but at the same time it would be important for the Finns to get the West Germans into some kind of agreement about the Baltic that would make this inland sea a part of a nuclear-free area. The Finns' active furtherance of conferences and projects for the prevention of the contamination of the Baltic— Finland was the first country to ratify the 1974 Helsinki agreement on the prevention of pollution of the Baltic, the signatories to which were the Soviet Union, Poland, Denmark, Sweden, Finland, and the two Germanies—must be seen not merely in the light of the actual issue dealt with but also in the light of Finnish hopes for a wider Baltic agreement, to be signed by both Germanies, that would relate more directly to Finland's own security needs. In any case, as we shall presently see, the desire for guarantees from Germany—which, being given, render even more improbable the need to implement the 1948 Treaty—has emerged in Finnish policy in another context.

In the meantime a certain urgency has been evident in the Finns' attitude to their key proposal for the creation of a North European nuclear-free zone. Apunen, Korhonen, Kalervo Siikala, and the chairman of the Security Policy Association in Finland, Reima

Luoto, have all indicated that further delay in fulfilling this proposal is most unwelcome,[29] for they fear the spread to Northern Europe of mini-nuclear weapons that will not need for their employment or deployment any vast installations.

The Finns' fear in this regard concerns in the first place Sweden. Reima Luoto has gone so far as to argue that it will be difficult for Swedish military potential to expand—which simply means keeping up with the currently changing arms-level—without introducing weapons of this kind. On the whole the Finns have feared for some time the possibility of a change in Sweden's own neutrality and recent statements made by the head of the Swedish defence forces, General Synnergren, have not been reassuring. According to reports in the Finnish press on 11 March 1975, Synnergren admitted the difficulties an unaligned state like Sweden had in keeping up with the arms level of the power blocs. He had earlier expressed apprehensions that the improved Finnish rail and road network would easily permit, in a conflict situation, of the transport of twelve Soviet divisions across Finland. As if to balance these concerns, the Swedes were prepared to sell their own Viggen fighters to NATO—a deal that has not come off—while the Swedish foreign minister, in a statement also reported in the Finnish press on the same date, admitted the necessity for some cooperation in weapon technology with NATO.

In the second place the Finns remain apprehensive about Norwegian attitudes. As far as mini-nuclear weapons are concerned, the Norwegian strategist J. J. Holst recently assured the Finns, in their own journal *Ulkopolitiikka*, no. 1, 1975, that the Pentagon is not considering any large-scale plans for their employment. But in the January 1975 issue of the Chatham House journal *International Affairs* Michael Brenner argued that, on the contrary, the Pentagon wanted the re-equipment of NATO forces with mini-nukes. How far, for example, will the need felt to protect the Norwegian maritime oilfields drive NATO into an attempt to intensify its role in Norway—and what then would be the corresponding reaction of the Soviet Union? It is not in the Finns' interest to see a stiffening of Soviet attitudes to North European problems, for this might easily lead to a division between the North European states themselves, a consequence of which for Finland might be the intensification of the military-political relationship with the Soviet Union.

Further, as far as the Vienna Mutual Force Reduction discussions have been concerned—discussions from which Finland as a neutral state is excluded—a natural wariness from the Finnish side has been evinced. The Finns have feared that the 'salami theory', according to which a reduction in Central European military commitments might be followed by a compensatory expansion in North European military commitments, might turn out to be only too true.

In the light of these problems the Finnish proposal for a nuclear-free North European zone, as well as the other projects the Finns have put forward for neutralizing Northern Europe, can be understood as attempts to maintain the status quo. The Finnish answer to the Norwegian charge that such measures would tend rather to *weaken* the status quo is contained in the proposal to have Northern Europe guaranteed by the superpowers. This is in line with general Finnish policy to secure guarantees of collective security.

The German package-deal

For many years the Finnish government refused to have full diplomatic relations either with West or East Germany. During his explanatory visit to France in October–November 1962 Kekkonen, in an interview with *Le Monde*, referred to Finland's German policy with the simple explanation that ' la Finlande s'est efforcée, conformément à sa politique de neutralité, de se maintenir en dehors des conflits entre les grandes puissances'. This Finnish policy of avoiding, seemingly, the favouring of either of the two Germanies became one of the hallmarks of Finnish neutrality. It bolstered the image of Finnish neutrality, justifying it in terms of its original, pragmatic, non-partisan approach to one of the most vexing problems of European politics. Equally, however, as Kekkonen had said in France, the Finnish policy towards the two Germanies went to the heart of Finnish neutrality policy, which was based on avoiding conflicts of interest of the powers.

From the point of view of approach to the German question, the Finns, having only trade missions in Bonn and East Berlin, appeared, where the doctrine of neutrality was concerned, to have stolen a march on the Swedes, who had recognized Bonn but not East Berlin. In reality, however, the Finnish doctrine also favoured West Germany, for it was East Germany that was most hungry for the recognition of other states and was prepared for third states to recognize both Germanies in consequence—the exact opposite of the Finnish position.

On 10 September 1971 the Finnish government dramatically reversed its German policy and in a proposal to both German governments that soon became known as the 'German package' advocated recognition of both Germanies in return for certain favours from the German (both East and West) side—a 'deal' in fact. These favours consisted on the one hand of a demand for the recognition of Finnish neutrality policy and a promise not to use force or the threat of it in relations with Finland, and on the other hand of claims for legal and economic compensation for the destruction caused by German troops in Finland during the Finnish-German hostilities of 1944–5. In a communiqué issued on 11 September the Finnish government stressed that the signing of the treaties based on the 'package' was to take place simultaneously with both Germanies and in a radio and television speech of the same day President Kekkonen stated that the 'package' was to be considered as a whole, that is, it was not going to be possible to bargain independently about parts of it.

This somewhat grand approach was not alleviated by the manner in which the Finnish proposal was presented to the Germanies and other states. There was no prior consultation with East and West Germany: the major powers had no wind of it either. In justifying the absence of consultation, Ahti Karjalainen, then prime minister, speaking in Finland on 20 September and Yrjö Väänänen, the Finnish consul-general in West Germany, speaking in Bonn ten days earlier, both implied that if there had been consultation the German states would have tried to alter the proposal and at that point negotiations would have already begun. Still, there seemed to be something precipitate in the Finnish action. Karjalainen stressed, however, that the Finns were laying down no timetable for the negotiations: they had simply wanted to get their proposals put forward in good time before the two Germanies themselves came to final agreement, when, according to the Finnish viewpoint, it might have been too late for the Finns to get for their demands the attention they deserved—they would be 'drowned in the general hubbub'.

But then more unsavoury aspects of Finnish precipitate action began to come to light. Not merely had the Parliamentary Foreign Affairs Committee been kept uninformed, but the foreign minister himself had not, due to illness, been present at the cabinet meeting which announced the 'package' to the world. Now the foreign minister was Väinö Leskinen, the repentant Tannerite Social Democrat, and the Social Democratic Party bureau had itself been working on a plan for a German 'package-deal' which Hyvärinen and Korhonen now trumped by getting their own version through the Foreign Ministry. In addition, it soon began to be bruited around that one of the reasons for the urgency in presenting the proposal to the Germans and other states was that the foreign minister himself had talked about the project already in the Copenhagen meeting of Nordic foreign ministers held earlier in the month (and it should be remembered that this particular Finnish démarche was not the product of joint Nordic cooperation, as one of the points of difference between Finnish and the rest of Scandinavian foreign policy had been in the attitude to the recognition of the Germanies).[30] As if to emphasize the importance of these party-political matters in foreign policy Karjalainen, in his speech of 20 September, had found it relevant to point out that the distinction between foreign and internal politics was as firm as a line drawn in water and that attitudes typical of the Centre Party, to which of course Ahti Karjalainen belonged, could be seen reflected in Finnish foreign policy. The truth was that much of the background to the German 'package-deal' mirrored the half-hidden conflict between the Centre and Social Democratic Parties, the leading parties of the coalition government, for control of foreign policy. Through the Socialist International, which met in Helsinki in May 1971, the Finnish Social Democrats had for some years been cultivating relations with the German Social Democratic Party, and the Helsinki meeting, addressed by Willy Brandt, Bruno Kreisky, Harold Wilson, Denis Healey, as well as Northern European leaders, was on the whole a successful act of policy for the Finnish SDP, which was additionally exempted by Soviet press organs from their attacks upon the International's member parties.

Thus the Centre Party's special relationship with Finnish foreign policy was being challenged and the subsequent political in-fighting in Finland undoubtedly accounted for some of the clumsiness that lay behind the presentation to the world of the German 'package-deal'. The lack of preparation and the insufficiency of elucidation, once the 'package' had been launched, were both partly due to these internal political factors.

It became at once apparent that whatever the professed Finnish desire to show equality of approach to the two Germanies might mean to the Finns, it meant something else to the Germans themselves. As early as 20 September the East Germans had replied by expressing their willingness to begin negotiations as soon as possible. On 27 September the West German reply came: it said that the Bonn government was looking into the matter—in short, the Bonn government wished to shelve it temporarily. The governmental reaction in West Germany was closely reflected in the press. Typical was the comment of the *Kölnischer Zeitung* of 13 September, which said that while the Finns assumed that the negotiations between East and West Germany were in their final stages, they were in fact only in the initial stages. These matters, the West German press as a whole believed, were still to be considered as internal German matters. And so it became clear that if the earlier Finnish approach to relations with the Germanies, i.e. full diplomatic relations with neither, leaned if anything to the West German position, the new solution favoured East Germany. Elsewhere in Western Europe, *The Economist*, for example—in an article of 18 September calling Finland 'too eager a beaver'—described the Finnish démarche as a challenge to Bonn and recalled uneasily the Finnish endeavours to get into closer relations with the Comecon countries. Superficially seen, therefore, it was easy for West European opinion to draw the conclusion that Finland was favouring the Soviet bloc, intentionally or unintentionally. Nevertheless, in the light of the Finnish government's own reticence, Western press comments were invariably diverse and highly speculative.

As far as the Soviet response was concerned a certain initial coolness was observable. On 12 September *Pravda* reproduced the Finnish communiqué and added that the démarche had been welcomed in the German People's Republic. It was left for the Finnish defence minister, Kristian Gestrin,[31] to discover during his visit to Moscow later in the month that the Soviet reaction was favourable to the démarche. More enthusiasm was shown elsewhere in Eastern Europe and the Poles pointed out that Finland was already championing the East German participation in the June 1972 Stockholm conference on the environment.[32]

In the subsequent months the pace of response from the East German side was consistently quicker than from West Germany. In November a prominent member of the East German Communist Party, Herman Axen, arrived in Finland as head of a delegation that came to see both the Finnish Communist Party and the Finnish government. Axen was received by President Kekkonen, Prime Minister Teuvo Aura, and Foreign Minister Olavi Mattila (Finland then had a temporary civil servants' caretaker government). Axen's visit and reception were regretted in West Germany. By July 1972 strong rumours were prevalent that Finland intended to 'untie' the 'package' if progress were not made soon[33] and in Rostock the former East German foreign minister, Lothar Bolz, accused West Germany of attempting to blackmail Finland with the threat that if Finland went ahead on its own to normalize relations with East Germany Finland's hosting of the European Security Conference might be called into question.[34] There was a double-irony in Bolz's remarks, for the logical conclusion to draw would have been that West Germany favoured after all an equitable 'package-deal'. But the West Germans were in no obvious hurry to put this viewpoint over and in September the Finns initialled an agreement with East Germany by which the East Germans professed 'respect' for Finland's neutrality policy. The unconscious irony in Bolz's remark about the Security Conference now seemed to have become even more magnified, for one of Finland's purposes in proposing the original 'package-deal' on equal terms to both Germanies had been to ensure the holding of the European Security Conference in Helsinki with the full participation of both German states.

Nevertheless, if anything, it now became evident that it was Finland that was able to put on the pressure. The agreement initialled between Finland and East Germany on 6 September 1972 provided for the opening of diplomatic relations between the two states. The West Germans could not afford to lag behind and on 7 January 1973 diplomatic relations were established between Finland and both Germanies, the first phase of the Security Conference being held in Helsinki in the following summer. But the 'package' has indeed had to be 'untied'. In the continuing negotiations both with East and West Germany the matter of compensation for the Wehrmacht's scorched earth policy in Lapland has for the moment been shelved. On the other hand by September 1974, in a joint Finnish-West German communiqué, the West German government agreed to 'respect' Finnish neutrality policy (the original Finnish demand had been for 'recognition' of such a policy) and both states agreed to renounce the threat and use of force in their relations. The East Germans had already agreed the latter. Soon after this communiqué was issued, *Die Welt* attacked Finland as a state subordinate in its policy to the Soviet Union, which in turn provoked a bitter reply from the Finnish foreign minister, Karjalainen.[35]

The fact that from the inception of the German 'package-deal' the Finnish government miscalculated both the tempo and temper of West Germany,[36] that the Americans had to be reassured that Finland was not making any radical departure from its hitherto careful neutrality policy,[37] and that in the end the Western powers chose to adopt a kindly, understanding attitude to the rapidly-fragmenting 'package', ought not to obscure from view the fundamental aims of Finnish foreign policy that were laid down in the proposal of 10 September 1971. Even though the 'package' was concocted in the light of the final abandonment by West Germany of the Hallstein doctrine in 1969 and at a time when the Finns were convinced that Willy Brandt's own Ostpolitik was going on to ever greater triumphs (and they were right), it was Willy Brandt himself who emphasized in an interview with *Der Spiegel* published on 27 September 1971 that the point of departure for the Finns was the recently-concluded Berlin agreement; an agreement, he stressed, that was made by the Four Powers but not the Germanies. In detail the Finnish proposal asked for 'the renunciation of the use or threat of force—whether on the part of a government being a party to the treaty or of some other country acting from within the territory of the Contracting Parties'. This stipulation would have associated the Four Powers—who had troops on German soil—with the treaty. Once again therefore the Finns were searching for some kind of guarantee, both from West and East. Not merely would this stipulation have meant a renunciation of force from the NATO side, but the Soviet Union too would have bound itself in some way not to use force against Finland, at least as far as its troops in East Germany were concerned. Thus Finland's hasty démarche contained a wealth of ambitions and reached into realms that, though central to Finland's security policy, were still of a highly speculative nature.

At any rate, in achieving a measure of acceptance of their neutrality policy and a pledge of the renunciation of the use or threat of force from both the Germanies, the Finns have succeeded once more in rendering less likely the implementation of the 1948 Treaty, as several perceptive journalists realized at the time the 'package-deal' was first launched.[38] Indeed, the Finnish foreign minister even went so far as to say in a radio interview that the German 'package' rendered the 1948 Treaty unnecessary, a view he had to recant by emphasizing later that of course it did not.[39] A written declaration by a Warsaw Pact state, i.e. East Germany, that it respected Finnish neutrality policy was, however, something of an achievement, for with no other Warsaw Pact state do the Finns have such a written avowal. It was indeed rumoured that the Finns tried to get a recognition of their neutrality written into the renewed Treaty of Friendship, Cooperation and Mutual Assistance with the Soviet Union in 1970, although Kekkonen denied that such an attempt was made.[40] A large number of Finns wanted the attempt to be made, and the idea of it certainly fitted the general outlook of Finland's foreign policy decision-makers at this time. In this sense the German 'package' has ultimately afforded the Finns a certain compensation.

Discussion of the important connections the 'package' has with Finnish economic policy will be left to the next chapter. The culminating feature of the Finnish policy of seeking guarantees for security now merits attention.

The European Security Conference—security by patent

At one and the same time the Finns were hosting the SALT talks, proposing the German 'package-deal', and seeking to promote the European Security Conference. In a statement referring to all three measures, which he made on 13 October 1971, the Finnish foreign minister Väinö Leskinen had emphasized that they had all issued from the growing détente in Europe and the rest of the world. Though Leskinen did not say so, this connection with the fundamental mood of détente in Europe was vital for the Finns. Without it they could have taken no initiatives in these matters, for then they might have been involved in 'the conflicting interests of the great powers' and damaged the image of their neutrality. Thus once again in the last resort the success of Finnish policy rests upon its acceptability by all the leading powers. Conversely, once the leading powers do accept Finnish policy, it becomes somewhat hollow to turn round and accuse the Finns of suffering from *Finnlandisierung*, since all the major features of Finnish policy rest upon the conviction of a basic community of interests between the leading powers themselves as well as between the smaller states.

Leskinen maintained that the Finnish policy-makers made a study of the situation in Europe in the spring of 1969 and came to the conclusion that the cold war was over and acted—in regard to the promotion of the Security Conference—in that light. The question therefore from the Finnish side is one of making a definite calculation of a mood and its tempo. We have seen that in respect of the two Germanies the Finns showed themselves to be too precipitate and to have overestimated the speed of détente. Yet something was gained by the Finns out of it. Has their involvement with the Security Conference turned out to be of a rather similar nature?

Two sharply contrasting attitudes are to be met with in the Finnish attitude to the European Security Conference. In the first place a great deal of idealism was sparked off in the Finnish press, radio and TV, and in Finnish public opinion by the conference, the first session of which was held in Helsinki in the summer of 1973 and the final session again in Helsinki in the summer of 1975. This idealism was part of the general back-up for Finnish foreign policy that existed among all ranks of society and affected all shades of political opinion. It was the emergence of that consensus so desired —and striven for—by the policy-makers themselves. But it is difficult to believe that the policy-makers had simply manipulated the people. The former, too, shared some of the latter's enthusiasm. Reputable historians compared the Security Conference with the Congress of Vienna in 1815[41]—two years before, *Time*, in its issue of 7 July 1975, chose to do likewise. Leading Finnish diplomats threw in Versailles for good measure.[42]

In the second place, however, Finnish policy regarding the Security Conference was based upon a continuum of *Realpolitik*. Essentially this meant that the starting-point for Finnish policy was no different at the end of the 60s from what it had been in 1954 when the Soviet Union raised for the first time the question of a European Security Conference. Finland's answer then, delivered to the Soviet government by the Finnish minister in Moscow Åke Gartz, on 18 November 1954, had been that Finland would participate in a conference of this kind provided all states interested, whether large or small, and irrespective of their social and political systems, would also join in: when they did not, due to Western opposition, it was impossible for the Finns to consider participation. The same principle lay at the heart of the Finnish note of 5 May 1969, which was addressed not merely to the governments of the European states including both East and West Germany but also to the United States and Canada. These latter states had not been invited to a conference in the Warsaw Pact note of 18 March 1969, though the subsequent NATO communiqué on this question of 11 April 1969 had stressed the necessity of negotiating with 'all governments whose participation would be necessary to achieve a political settlement in Europe'. The Finnish note, which reflected viewpoints already voiced at the North European foreign ministers' meeting at Copenhagen on 23–24 April, thus leaned to the NATO viewpoint in drawing in the United States and Canada, but it also served as a means of enabling the Warsaw Pact governments to accept these two states. In any case both in 1954 and in 1969 and after the Finnish attitude was that all states concerned should be represented, but the viewpoint expressed by the Finnish diplomat Yrjö Väänänen that the only difference in 1969 was that the Finns now proposed Helsinki as the venue of the conference is inadequate:[43] in 1969 the Finns openly wanted and worked for the inclusion of the two major North American states (in July 1970 President Kekkonen went to the United States to talk about the Security Conference). Such moves the Finns could not have contemplated in 1954.

Hand in hand with the insistence on the participation of all states with a stake in European affairs went a Finnish belief in the importance of having as much preliminary agreement as possible before the conference formally convened, while at the conference decisions were to be reached by consensus. These ideas were not dreamt up by the Finns—indeed it was necessary to coin a new and not altogether successful expression in the Finnish language to explain what the idea of consensus was to the Finnish people.[44] But the advantage of consensus was manifold. No open conflicts would occur, even the embarrassment of having to take sides by voting would be spared. And on top of this the minimal achievements of the conference would be beyond controversy as far as the states were concerned. Finally, a successful Security Conference, based on consensus between East and West, and partly sponsored by and hosted by the Finns, would enormously increase the prestige of Finnish foreign policy in the eyes of the Finnish people. If a consensus about the goals of Finnish policy already existed (even before the word had been translated into Finnish), this would now be confirmed and the unity of the Finnish people once more fostered through a devotion to neutrality with all its merits. Kekkonen's concept of neutrality as a way of life with internal significance has already been noted. He talked much about it in 1969 and the succeeding years. Not even the most disgruntled Communist in Finland could object to a Finnish neutrality that helped the Soviet Union to the conference table on the latter's own terms. For after a rather slow start in 1966, when in the joint Finnish-Soviet communiqué of 18 June that concluded Kosygin's visit to Finland both countries agreed on the usefulness of a Security Conference, the mutual admiration between Finland and the Soviet Union on each country's efforts to promote the conference had rapidly grown by 1969, and the Warsaw Pact communiqué issued in Prague in October 1969 singled out the Finnish initiative for praise.

And yet Finnish Security Conference policy remains a part of

Finland's own policy to provide for a security system in Europe that will, without upsetting the Soviet Union, diminish the need and occasion for an intrusive Soviet presence, especially military, in the rest of Europe. Only the archives and memoirs may finally reveal what was the ultimate spur to Finnish initiative in this question. For although from 1966 onwards the Finns worked in a group of small states that were promoting the Conference—a group consisting of NATO, Warsaw Pact, neutral, and non-aligned states[45] that had become known by 1967 as 'the Group of Ten'—the Finns did not throw themselves wholeheartedly into this work until the spring of 1969. It is not inconceivable that the events of the previous summer in Czechoslovakia were an important factor in urging on the Finns— opinion in Finland strongly identified with the Czechs, and the Finnish Communist Party condemned the entry of Soviet troops. On the other hand after the Czechoslovak crisis the Soviet authorities were in some need of help in making gestures of reconciliation to the West. Finland, a small state, could help the Soviet Union to recover some of the prestige it had lost by the shabby treatment of another small state, Czechoslovakia. In this situation Czechoslovakia's loss became Finland's gain. Not that the Finns forgot the Czechs either. Speaking in Prague on 4 October 1969 President Kekkonen referred to the strength of national feeling among what he called 'small and medium-large states' for whom 'security is a vital issue of national existence'. He went on: 'The right national feeling is above all a knowing search for the nation's own national role in international contacts, in a way which is constructive and does not give rise to conflicts'. The Finns had evidently been wiser than their hosts.

In their wisdom the Finns also knew that while the atmosphere in Europe had deteriorated after the Czechoslovak crisis, as the foreign minister Karjalainen admitted in an interview with the Austrian paper *Die Presse* on 4 November 1969, the broad desire in Europe for détente remained. Indeed, by 1971 foreign minister Väinö Leskinen was arguing that the handling of the Czechoslovak crisis by the NATO and Warsaw Pact powers was a triumph of European understanding.[46] All these elements contributed to a situation that was ripe for Finland's own 'bridge-building' efforts, the 'bridge-builder's' role, along with the doctor's role (the latter first enunciated by Kekkonen in his UN speech of 19 October 1961), being the favourite definitions of Finland's function in international activity. In February 1970 Finland appointed Ralf Enckell as roving ambassador to the European states and his task over the next few months was to persuade the states to view the conference positively, to make initial preparations with them, and in particular to press the claims of Helsinki as a host-city for the conference.

As to what the Finns themselves wanted on the agenda of the conference, a certain coyness generally descended on Finnish spokesmen when they were asked this question. It became obvious, however, that at heart what they wanted was confirmation of the status quo in Europe, the objectives of what came to be known in the conference as Basket I, and in particular the agreed principles of the 1973 Helsinki Consultations, especially principles (ii) 'refraining from the threat or use of force', (iii) 'inviolability of frontiers', (iv) 'territorial integrity of states', (v) 'peaceful settlement of disputes', and (vi) 'non-intervention in internal affairs', all of which were embodied in the final declaration of principles of the conference in 1975. As far as the Finns were concerned, there should be no contentious argument about these principles—they were to be established for future reference, and it was prudent to avoid debating them in terms of contemporary problems. This the representatives of the Baltic émigré organizations found out in trying to crash the Helsinki Conference discussions in the summer of 1973: 'inviolability of frontiers' and 'territorial integrity of States' meant at this moment of time the same to the Finns as it did to the Soviet Union —there was to be no calling into question of existing arrangements. It was no coincidence that when on 25 April 1971 the Finnish Conservative newspaper *Uusi Suomi* published an article on 'The Baltic Question in the Present-Day World' (referring to Estonia, Latvia, and Lithuania) in the light of the Soviet attempt to secure recognition of the status quo in Europe, the Finnish foreign minister Väinö Leskinen summoned the editor of the newspaper to the ministry for reprimand (however friendly).[47]

But as the Finns saw the conference approaching realization, it seemed more and more apparent that if there were going to be obstacles to the general agreement on principles about territorial integrity and inviolability of frontiers the main source of tension was not going to be the half-forgotten Balts, nor the Irish, nor the West *in toto* as it formulated its viewpoint that the inviolability of frontiers meant that they could not be changed by force but only by peaceful negotiation: the main source of tension was likely to be the still unclear position of divided Germany. In 1969 Karjalainen had told the *Die Presse* interviewer that Germany would be the 'central problem' for the conference, but his reply assumed that it would nevertheless be on the agenda. By 1971 it had become evident to the Finns that differences between the great powers were affecting the question of the Security Conference agenda in regard to which the Finns, in their neutrality and expressed benevolence to both sides, now refused to take a stand. It was, however, clear to the Finns that the German question at least ought to be brought to some kind of conclusion before the conference met. This was not merely a question of getting both states represented at the conference, but of removing a source of disagreement beforehand—preventive politics in fact. The success of Brandt's Ostpolitik became vital to the Finns, and part of their own feverish haste over their German 'package-deal' can be explained against the background of their concern to avoid squabbling at the conference.

The nearer the Security Conference came to realization the more the Finns strove to ensure that controversy would not break out once it was held. The Finnish leaders, who travelled frequently to the European states, did not want any demonstrations of protest arising from East European states either, and endeavoured before-hand to cool down the Romanians, who might be suspected of wishing to demonstrate the claims of small states too openly against the Soviet Union at the conference. The scene on the opening day of the conference in June 1973, when the Finnish chairman Richard Tötterman closed the proceedings after a brief, formal opening, immediately to be followed by a Romanian objection, may be regarded as typical of the contrasting attitudes.

One project the Finns wished to discuss, both at the time of the Security Conference and in connection with it was, of course, the nuclear-free zone plan for Northern Europe. Through this project the Finns had an obvious interest in the political-military dis-cussions of the First Basket. But many of the more important matters, namely troops reductions, have been hived off to the Mutual Force Reduction negotiations in Vienna, where Finland as a neutral cannot be represented. Kekkonen has stated that there is 'a logical connection' between the Security Conference and the Vienna discussions, but the Finnish Foreign Office denies press rumours that Finland, like Sweden, wants the neutral states to be consulted in connection with the latter talks. Instead the Finns claim to have concentrated their efforts, this time admittedly with other neutrals and states like Yugoslavia and Cyprus, on finding compromise formulas in the Geneva discussions that will satisfy the states of both the major blocs. This work, for example in sub-committee C, involves handling military questions—the so-called confidence-building measures, such as notification of troop manœuvres. The chairmanship of the Finnish delegate Klaus Törnudd has been much appreciated in these detailed Geneva discussions. But what does all this unspectacular, if useful, work add up to for the Finns? Max Jakobson did this kind of thing well in the United Nations, as we shall see in the final chapter, and the end-product of that was one of the most ambitious and unsuccessful moves Finnish foreign policy has made in recent years.

This time there are to be no bold démarches. In spite of their idealism, the Finns do not intend to depart again from the funda-mental caution with which they have traditionally approached foreign-political issues. Nevertheless their basic aim is to involve their country in a series of multilateral relationships in which a neutral state can play a role that in no way diminishes its neutrality. But the role is not played for its own sake. It is the endeavour of Finnish policy to see a Europe bound together by a series of cross-relationships that will overlap not only countries of different political, economic, and social systems—in the best tradition of peaceful coexistence—but will also overlap the blocs, whether political, economic, or military. In this connection the ultimate out-come of the Security Conference, the declaration of principles signed in Helsinki by the representatives of the participant states on 1 August 1975, produced a special bonus for the Finns. As a result of the exertions of the Swiss, the right of a country to neutrality was confirmed, and, as already noted, such international recognitions of neutrality are highly valued by the Finns. At the same time the right of states to enter into or not to enter into both bilateral and multi-lateral agreements was also written into the declaration.

However much the Finns in their realism believe that the essential condition for peace in the world is to be found in the relationship between the United States and the Soviet Union, with its con-comitant balance of terror, such a viewpoint hardly commits the Finns, as citizens of a state declaredly neutral, to regard military blocs in a particularly favourable light. In a classic statement on Finland's position delivered at the UN General Assembly as early as 12 December 1957, Finland's delegate Ralph Enckell described Finland as a state that belonged to no bloc or combination of states and would be happier if the terms 'east' and 'west' could simply be regarded as geographical expressions. In his lecture of 16 June 1971 to the Lahti Summer University the then foreign minister, Väinö Leskinen, returned even more openly to this theme. Having referred, *inter alia*, to the planned Security Conference, Leskinen went on to look forward to a Europe that was divided neither by the Cold War nor yet completely integrated in one system. There was to be a 'mixed collection of states in different political-economic associations'. He hoped that this development would not in the end lead to new blocs.

In the same lecture Leskinen stressed the importance of founding new organs in Europe for security issues as well as forums for discussions of mutual European problems. In the Inter-Parliamentary Union Conference which was held in Helsinki in January 1973, the president of the Finnish Group, Dr J. Virolainen, a member of the Finnish cabinet and chairman of the Centre Party, gave support to the idea of a Euroforum for the parliaments of Europe. And so when it came to the Security Conference itself the Finns had a strong interest in the contents of the Fourth Basket—the follow-up, the creation if possible of a permanent machinery for European security. It is hardly surprising that they have already quietly favoured ideas like that of the Swiss 'tribunal d'arbitrage' to which European states could submit their disputes, a proposal that has not raised much interest from the Soviet or NATO sides.

In spite of a certain identity of interest that Finns have with other neutral states and in spite of the existence of some degree of cooperation with other neutrals at Geneva, the Finns wish to prevent the growth of the idea that a bloc of neutrals is in formation. The Finns like to stress that their own channels of information are much wider than those provided simply by an association with other neutrals. For instance, through the framework of Northern European Cooperation the Finns are in contact with two NATO countries, Norway and Denmark, and with one EEC country, Denmark, and it should be remembered that the foreign ministers of these Northern states meet twice a year to discuss problems of mutual interest. In addition, the Finns pursue a policy of sending representatives and observers to various European organizations. Though, for reasons dating back to the Cold War, they are not, for example, in the Council of Europe, they still participate in the work of the Council's subordinate organizations, even arranging conferences for these organizations in Finland.

Against this background of already-existing multilateral contacts the Finns feel that they are in a favourable position to act in turn as 'contact men' and mediators of ideas in international negotiations like those of the Security Conference. This aspect of active neutrality has won for the Finns a certain admiration from the Swiss, who have even come to wonder whether their own form of neutrality should be considered rather more in terms of policy and rather less in terms of defined and absolute status. Jealousy has been more in evidence from the Austrian side, where doubts have been expressed in view of Finland's close relations with the Soviet bloc.[48] But it is in this, too, that the Finns claim to have special advantages of a positive value to both sides. For several years, for example, the Finnish Social Democratic Party has been promoting in the Socialist International the idea of establishing relations between the West and North European Social Democratic Parties and the workers' parties of Eastern Europe, and at present contacts are in fact developing between the Finnish Social Democratic Party and the Hungarian Socialist Workers' Party. These links, which Finland's Social Democrat prime minister, Kalevi Sorsa, sought to foster on his visit to Hungary in September 1974, assist—according to the Finnish viewpoint—the main drive towards European security. For Sorsa went to Hungary primarily to urge on the next and final session of the Security Conference. The Finns had already hoped to have the final session in Helsinki in autumn 1974 and then, when this seemed to be beyond hope, they looked round for allies to work with them to get the conference sitting as early as possible. Hungary, a Warsaw Pact country that was not, however, represented at the Mutual Force Reduction talks in Vienna, and therefore was in this respect in a parallel position to Finland, was an obvious contact-point. Relations between Finland and Hungary were good on the grounds also of the recently concluded KEVSOS trade agreement, which will be dealt with at greater length in chapter 4, but which it is important to see as a factor in Finnish Security Conference activity, for in regard to this and similar KEVSOS agreements made by Finland with other East European states (see below, p. 121), the Finns are apt to think that they have created model agreements that can be of value in forming new economic relationships between states with different economic systems. This has for them relevance to the Second Basket of the Security Conference, where economic, technical, and environmental matters are discussed.

The bonds of neutrality

The similarity between the Finnish and Soviet attitudes to the

4

Security Conference is striking. The Finnish predilection for a weakening and transformation of the blocs could well have been summed up in the words of the Soviet commentator A. Bovin in *Izvestia* of 4 July 1972, according to which the aim of the conference is the replacement of blocs by 'an effective system of multilateral guarantees and obligations backed by corresponding institutional mechanisms'. Significantly, shortly after Sorsa returned from Hungary, where (as noted) his main object had been to work for the swift continuance of the next stage of the Security Conference, Leonid Brezhnev, speaking in East Germany on 6 October 1974, at the twenty-fifth anniversary celebrations of the East German state, blamed the delay in resuming the Security Conference session on the Western objections raised in connection with the Third Basket, namely questions of human contact and exchange of ideas.

Here is the crux of the problem for the Finns. So keen have they appeared to work for a Security Conference that they have been inclined to overlook the magnitude of the problems involved in the exchange of information and personal contacts, matters concerning which they certainly do not bear any wide responsibility. But in answer to the question put at the beginning of the previous section, it can be said that the Finns again overestimated the speed at which détente was occurring. In regard to this, their own internal self-censorship—seen at its clearest in the attitude towards Solzhenitsyn's *Gulag Archipelago*—hardly helps in the formation of a correct picture of the concerns of the world outside Finland. Particularly does this apply to Western Europe, the point where serious reservations about the Security Conference have been made.

Nevertheless the weight of evidence is that the Finns have pursued a policy on the Security Conference that directly reflects their own national interests. Part of the effectiveness of this policy stems from Finnish neutrality policy, but neutrality, like prosperity, brings with it its own problems. If neutrality is a way of life that has internal significance, it is not without its damaging aspect either. The real reason for Finnish self-censorship is often said to lie in the behaviour of the Stalinist wing of the Finnish Communist Party, who will immediately inform the Soviet embassy if anything derogatory to the Soviet Union is published in Finland and thus compel protest from the Soviet side. The question is wider than this, however, and the publishing house that could have published but did not publish *The Gulag Archipelago* is said to have feared a negative reaction from all its potential Leftist writers. In any case the desire to keep Finland's own internal politics on an even keel, to create a front of unanimity that Kekkonen himself has regarded as a vital factor in the success of Finnish policy vis-à-vis the Security Conference,[49] has run counter to a frank consideration of some of the most compelling issues of the Security Conference that are the contents of the Third Basket. In a world in which foreign policy deals more and more with questions of the transmission of ideas, freedom of movement, economic and technological bargaining, a policy of neutrality becomes trickier to pursue, and in pursuing it the state concerned may easily find that its endeavours are brought to a halt.

In spite of this, the trend of development in Europe remains broadly favourable to the Finns, and in this favourable development they claim a modest credit. Their primary motivation has so far been seen to be one of security policy—Kekkonen remarked in the course of a lecture he gave on 29 November 1965 that 'it is natural that every state devotes incessant efforts to consolidating its political position'. But security for the Finns is also very much bound up with economic policy. From this point of view the trend in Europe—including here, too, the contents of the Second Basket of the Security Conference—have been favourable to the aspirations of the controlling elements of Finnish society.

Notes

1. Thögersen, p. 121.
2. The importance for the Finns of avoiding the implementation of Article 2 was stressed at the time of the crisis by Prof. Erik Castren in *Uusi Suomi*, 1 Nov 1961.
3. Jakobson, *Finnish neutrality*, p. 98. This view was corrected by P. Krymov and K. Golovanov, 'Finland's foreign policy', *Int. Affairs* (Moscow), Oct 1969.
4. Apunen, pp. 171 and 173.
5. Prime Minister J. Virolainen in *UPLA* 1965, pp. 30–1; Kekkonen, ibid., 1969, p. 111.
6. On this see the editorial in *Talouselämä* (Helsinki), 6 Mar 1969.
7. H. Hakovirta, *Suomen turvallisuuspolitiikka* (Helsinki, 1971), quoted in D. Anckar, 'Nytolkningar av Finlands neutralitet', *Hufvudstadsbladet*, 20 Mar 1974.
8. Soviet statements quoted in T. W. Wolfe, *Soviet power and Europe 1945–70* (Baltimore, 1970), pp. 199–200.
9. Šejna's revelations of Soviet contingency plans were first published in *Paris Match*, 14 Aug 1971, and continued later in the year—as far as the Soviet Union's North European plans were concerned—in the Swedish journal *Se*. The latter information was reproduced in part in the Finnish Rightist journal *Express*, no. 1, 1972. Capt. R. Wiksten's article in *Uusi Maailma*, 16 Mar 1972, argues that Šejna underestimates the strength of Scandinavian and Finnish resistance.
10. Written by Lt.-Col. J. Ruutu.

11. Unpublished paper, *Prof. Jan-Magnus Janssonin asiantuntijalausunto parl. puolustuskomitealle*, p. 6.
12. Broms, *Suomen puolueettomuus (Parivartio)*, p. 5.
13. P. Lyon, *Neutralism* (Leicester, 1963), pp. 97–8.
14. *Helsingin Sanomat*, 5 and 15 Jan 1968.
15. *Kansan Uutiset*, 10 Jan 1968.
16. Hyvärinen, 'Puolueettomuuden valtioiden turvallisuus ongelma', *Tiede ja ase* (Helsinki), 23 (1965), pp. 9, 22–3, and 26. On Törngren's statement, see G. A. Gripenberg, *Neutralitetstanken i Finlands politik* (Stockholm, 1960), p. 5; *Parlamentaarisen puolustuskomitean mietintö* (Helsinki, 1971), p. 22.
17. These rumours are mentioned by Ørvik, pp. 171–2.
18. Hakovirta, pp. 63–4, 104, 107–8, 110, and 115.
19. Jansson's preface to the speeches of Kekkonen published in *Neutrality* (London, 1970), ed. T. Vilkuna, p. 9.
20. Korhonen in *Suomi toisen maailmansodan jälkeen*, p. 21. For a more traditional view from a Centre Party politician see J. Virolainen, *UPLA*, 1965, pp. 30–1.
21. *Hufvudstadsbladet*, 7 Apr 1974.
22. The edited version is in *UPLA* 1969, pp. 283–4. The fuller version is in *Helsingin Sanomat*, 25 Jan 1969.
23. The idea is also referred to in Pajunen's book *Sarjatulta* (Helsinki, 1966), pp. 72–3.
24. Quoted by Brundtland, *Cooperation and Conflict*, 2 (1966), p. 55.
25. e.g. Hyvärinen's statement in *Uusi Suomi*, 5 Apr 1966. Brodin (*Finlands utrikespolitiska doktrin*, p. 63) has pointed to a certain ambivalence in Finnish official thinking about nuclear weapons.
26. *Ydin*, 3 (1974).
27. B. Broms, *A nuclear-free zone in Northern Europe—idealism or realism*? (Paper delivered to the California Seminar for Disarmament, Feb 1974).
28. *Aamulehti*, 8 Aug 1974.
29. *Helsingin Sanomat*, 7 July and 15 Sept 1974. Korhonen spoke to the Pugwash Conference in August 1974.
30. Some details of the alleged 'leak' will be found in *Helsingin Sanomat*, 18 Sept 1971.
31. Ibid., 19 Sept 1971.
32. *Suomi ulkomaiden lehdistössä* (Helsinki, 1971) for the Polish Agency Press statement of 13 Sept 1971.
33. *Helsingin Sanomat*, 11 July 1972.
34. Ibid., 10 July 1972.
35. Ibid., 29 Sept 1974.
36. Ibid., 13 July 1974.
37. Ibid., 18 Sept 1971; *Turun Sanomat*, 17 Sept 1971.
38. e.g. the *Bergens Tidende* account of 14 Sept 1971 in *Suomi ulkomaiden lehdistössä*.
39. *Helsingin Sanomat*, 22 Sept 1971.
40. Ibid., 23 May 1972.
41. e.g. Professor T. Polvinen's article 'ETYKin edeltäjät', *Yhteishyvä*, 5 July 1973.
42. R. Tötterman's speech of 14 June 1971 in *UPLA* 1971.
43. Y. Väänänen's speech of 22 May 1970, ibid., 1970.
44. The term coined was 'laaja suostumus'.
45. M. Palmer, *The prospects for a European Security Conference* (London, 1971), p. 10.
46. V. Leskinen's speech of 16 June 1971 is in *UPLA* 1971.
47. I am indebted to Pertti Poukka, the editor of *Uusi Suomi*, for communicating to me an account of this interview.
48. *Wochenpresse*, 14 Oct 1971 in *Suomi ulkomaiden lehdistössä*. On the criticism of *Die Presse* in 1973 see *Helsingin Sanomat*, 29 Jan 1973.
49. Significantly one of the young Conservative leaders, J. Vikatmaa, repeated this theme in the summer of 1974 (*Turun Sanomat*, 22 Aug 1974).

4 THE ECONOMICS OF NEUTRALITY

FINLAND, a country with a home-market of less than 5 million people, depends for its high standard of living upon foreign trade. According to a statement made in Brussels by the Finnish minister for foreign trade, Olavi Mattila, on 24 November 1970, 25 per cent of Finland's GNP is made up of the export of goods and services. Figures given in the Kansallis-Osake-Pankki's *Economic Review* (1975:1) show that as far as Finland's exports were concerned, in 1974 22·1 per cent were with the remaining EFTA countries, 43·3 per cent were with the EEC countries, and 17·2 per cent were with the Comecon countries. In regard to imports, 23·3 per cent were from the EFTA lands, 36·6 per cent were from the EEC, and 22·4 per cent were from the Comecon area. Of the individual countries trading with Finland, the most important in 1974 was the Soviet Union, closely followed by Sweden, with Britain and West Germany occupying third and fourth place respectively. These figures show that the bulk of Finland's trade is with the West. The prominence of the Soviet Union in Finland's foreign trade is, however, even more significant than might at first appear, since this trade is bilateral barter trade, by which, for example, an excess of imports in one year is corrected by additional exports in the succeeding year, so that Finland does not suffer from a balance-of-payments problem in regard to this trade.

In looking at the nature of Finland's export pattern, it will at once become apparent that the prosperity of the country is based upon a comparatively simple export structure. In 1974, 53 per cent of Finnish exports were from the wood, paper and pulp industry and of the remainder 25 per cent of all exports were supplied by the metal and engineering industry. Nevertheless, in spite of this simplicity in the country's export pattern, Finland's economy has undergone radical changes in the postwar world. The most striking of these has been the decline in the importance of agriculture, which as late as 1955 accounted for 24 per cent of the GNP and employed 35 per cent of the labour force, while by 1967 these figures had fallen to 15 and 25 per cent respectively—by 1970 indeed it was estimated that only 20 per cent of the labour force was employed in agriculture.[1] The reverse side of this fundamental change has been the growth of urbanization, the development of new industries, and the emergence of a more sophisticated pattern of consumption.

The Finnish economic historian Erkki Pihkala has discerned three major phases in the postwar pattern of his country's foreign trade.[2] In the immediate postwar years, i.e. in the period up to 1952, Finland's economy simply struggled to get back to prewar conditions. Paradoxically this occurred in conjunction with an actual growth in agriculture, for whereas the cultivated area ceded to the Russians by the armistice agreement was something like 270,000 hectares, the amount of new fields created in compensation by the refugees and others in the rest of Finland rose to 360,000 hectares.[3] Further, throughout this period the Finns were compelled to pay a heavy burden of war reparations in goods to the Soviet Union (the significance of which will be dealt with in more detail below). These reparations did not, of course, figure in the export statistics. Small wonder was it that by 1948 the level of Finnish exports had reached only three-quarters of the 1938 figure. Considering the limitations under which Finland's export trade was carried on, this was, however, something of an achievement. Understandably the bulk of Finnish exports were from the wood, paper, and pulp industry—between 85 and 90 per cent—and only 5 per cent of exports were of metal goods, though these goods loomed large in the reparations to the Soviet Union.

A second phase in the development of Finland's postwar export trade began around the year 1952 and continued till Finland's special agreement with EFTA in 1961. Two important factors in the beginning of this period were the final paying-off of reparations to the Soviet Union and Finland's participation in the boom conditions generated by the Korean War. The metal industry, which had supplied a significant part of the war reparations, now saw its share of exports rise automatically to 15 per cent of the whole, while correspondingly the share in the export pattern of the products of the wood, paper and pulp industry declined somewhat. With the ending of reparations the Soviet Union began to figure prominently as a country taking Finnish exports, for the connection first established by reparations was continued thereafter by normal trading relations, though on a bilateral barter basis. Immediately after the ending of reparations, Finnish trade with the Soviet Union formed approximately 20 per cent of the export pattern, roughly the equivalent of Finland's export trade to England. But by the end of the period the amount of exports to the Soviet Union had fallen to 15 per cent of the whole, and the Finns were trading increasingly with Western Europe—in 1960, for example, West Germany's share in Finland's exports had risen to over 12 per cent. This more confident export pattern went hand in hand with changes in the nature of Finland's imports. Finland had joined GATT in 1949 and throughout the 1950s import tariffs were consequently reduced, while in the middle 1950s the dismantling of the import licensing system began, to be followed in 1957 by a devaluation. The freeing of imports, which meant in particular a growth in the import of raw materials and capital goods needed for the expansion of Finnish industry, testified to the feeling among industrial and commercial circles that Finland's *export* industry was capable of seizing the opportunities that participation in a freer economic system allowed. In this period, which was, as it turned out, something of a preparatory stage for Finland's association with EFTA, Finland's balance-of-payments problem nevertheless began.

The third phase of development in the postwar history of Finnish foreign trade was inaugurated by the FINEFTA agreement of 1961. The agreement did not disturb Finnish trade with the Soviet Union in the light of the provisions of the 1947 commercial treaty between Finland and the Soviet Union. At the same time Finland had a special institutional framework for entering into association with EFTA, so that there could be no question of its participating in the work of a supranational power, which anyway by definition EFTA was not. This was reassuring to the Soviet government, as was the 'most-favoured-nation' status for Soviet goods, which shared in the tariff reductions gradually introduced under the FINEFTA agreement for EFTA imports to Finland. On the other hand the East European Socialist countries were not granted 'most-favoured-nation' status, and one of the indirect consequences of the FINEFTA agreement was a decline in Finnish trade with these latter countries. A slight fall was also actually witnessed in the percentage, though not in the volume, of Finnish trade with the Soviet Union.

In large measure due to the FINEFTA agreement, the 1960s saw some astonishing developments in the pattern of Finnish trade. As a matter of fact, while trade with the EFTA countries rose to over 50 per cent of the whole, trade with the UK, for example, declined during the EFTA period. This was more than compensated for by a

tremendous increase in trade with Finland's neighbour Sweden—
something that, due to the similarity of the traditional exports of
these two countries—had hardly been deemed possible. The fact
was that with the FINEFTA agreement the Finnish industrial
pattern had greatly diversified: a whole new range of exports,
known collectively as 'the new export', and comprising textiles,
furniture, glassware, etc., entered the picture, as well as an increasing variety of metal goods. By 1972 the volume of Finnish foreign
trade had more than doubled compared with the pre-FINEFTA
period. But a feature of this phenomenon was a growing import both
of goods for industry and consumer goods, and trade deficits
developed leading to a devaluation in 1967 that provided no long-
term solution to the problem of Finland's adverse balance of payments. Indeed, the indebtedness of Finland to the West has
increased to such an extent that one of the economic correspondents
of the *Helsingin Sanomat*, Eero Helkkula, writing on 8 July 1975,
asserted that no other Western industrial country was getting into
debt at so fast a rate as Finland.

For in the meantime Finland strengthened its relations with the
West by entering into a limited agreement with the EEC, which was
signed on 30 November 1973 and came into force the following year.
The significance of this will be discussed at greater length on
pp. 117-20. But it should be remembered that entering into an agreement with the EEC has not meant that Finland's relationship with
EFTA has been entirely superseded. Certain EFTA countries, notably Sweden, remained, like Finland, outside EEC membership, so
that between Finland and Sweden, to take but one example, the
EFTA relationship is retained. As already noted, more than 22 per
cent of Finland's exports still go to the EFTA countries and in 1974
Finnish metal exports to Sweden increased by over 60 per cent,
while total metal exports to the EFTA countries, running at about
40 per cent of the whole metal export, were considerably higher than
the share taken by the EEC countries, approximately 22 per cent.[4]
Finally, it should also be noted that on 16 May 1973 Finland signed
an agreement with the Comecon countries for cooperation in
technical and research fields in the first instance, but with the
ultimate object of charting the opportunities for planned specializa-
tion in exports between Finland and these countries. This agreement has been regarded as the natural consequence of earlier
bilateral agreements on technical and research collaboration between
Finland and individual Comecon countries[5] and it also marks the

development once more of widening commercial relations with the East European Socialist countries and not merely with the Soviet Union. Nevertheless, at the present time the agreement may be regarded as having an undoubted political significance as well, in the sense of being a token balance to the agreement contracted six months later with the EEC. As we have seen, Finland's export pattern still remains, in spite of the growing diversification begun during the EFTA period, relatively simple. But the fact that Finland has had carefully and distinctively to define its trading relations with the three economic organizations of Europe, namely the EEC, EFTA, and Comecon, inevitably makes Finnish economic policy one of some complexity.

The politics of economic policy

In the preceding chapters Finnish foreign policy has been seen as an outcome of a basic security policy drive. In a sense foreign policy has been trying to achieve the security that military policy cannot ensure. It must now be asked at what point Finnish foreign policy has to seek to fulfil objectives that the economic interests of the Finnish community cannot themselves achieve unaided. In this connection it may be observed that the concept of security policy in Finland is often widened to include questions of economic security and that this refers not merely to protection, say, of trade, but also to the economic security of the individual (security of employment).

Commercial policy at any rate is by official definition in Finland a part of foreign policy, but this in turn imposes restrictions on commercial policy. The latter cannot go against the fundamental goals of foreign policy, the preservation of neutrality and national security. As far as the political neutrality of the country is concerned, it therefore becomes something of a barrier to a free-ranging pursuit of economic interests. In practice this means that Finland cannot become a full member of a political-economic organization such as the EEC. Indeed, the Finns are not even associate members of the EEC, but from 1 January 1974 became partners in a free-trade agreement with the Community. The negotiations for this agreement, which began on 6 April 1970, shortly after Finland's withdrawal from the abortive Nordek project (see below, pp. 115-17), needed justification in Finland and were variously described as being due to 'economic necessity' or 'defensive' in nature.[6] They were justified in these terms so as to strengthen the government line that a free-trade agreement did not constitute an infringement of Finnish neutrality—there was to be no Finnish participation in the expansionist aims of a political-economic West European bloc. It is obvious here that this utilization of Finland's political neutrality is a safeguard against unfavourable repercussions from the Soviet Union, but if neutrality covers in this case an externally limiting factor on Finnish policy (i.e. the Soviet Union's negative reaction if Finland goes too far in its EEC relationship), this does not invalidate the broad advantages of neutrality for Finland's economic policy. Neutrality provides a certain safeguard that Finland can share in both major European economic systems and be directed by neither. It means at one and the same time being outside the systems and being involved with them.

Whereas in the nineteenth century Finns were interested in the concept of neutrality as a protective device for their trade in war-time—when the rest of the Russian empire might be at war with England—nowadays the main purpose of neutrality is to protect economic relations in peacetime. The growing emphasis in present-day Finnish foreign policy on commercial matters therefore represents a turning away to some extent from the traditional concerns of foreign policy, a desire to preserve the status quo against the breakdown of war, and instead foreign policy is concerning itself increasingly with finding solutions to the current problems of a rapidly developing pattern of economic alignments.

Finnish export interests want the state to ensure as open a world market as possible for Finnish goods and in other ways—as, for example, by the devaluations of 1957 and 1967—to aid exports. The state, in its turn, is highly responsive to this pressure. For one thing the state itself has a direct interest in exporting, for 32 per cent of the paper industry and 35 per cent of the metal industry is state-owned.[7] Further, the state Bank of Finland is actively concerned, as part of a general policy to foster a positive balance of payments, to promote exports by monetary policy measures, in time of need by devaluation. Its willingness to do this, i.e. to listen to the views of the major exporting interests rather than perceiving the often-negative effect of devaluation on the economy as a whole, has been brought into the open in a critical study written by some of the Bank's own junior officials and published by the Social Democratic Party.[8] These writers claim that the Bank, though a state organ, is too autonomous in its decision-making and should be made more answerable to the democratically-elected government.

But they also blame the Leftist members of the previous governments that have sanctioned devaluation. And here the problem becomes one of infinite complexity. The relationship, for example, between the Social Democratic Party and industry on the one hand, between the Centre Party (formerly Agrarians) and industry on the other, and then the relationship between the Social Democratic Party and the Centre Party—the two parties forming the mainstay of the present government coalition—is very fluid. Into this picture, too, must be projected the ever-latent conflict between SAK (the trade union movement) and MTK (the agricultural producers' associations).

One of the most significant events in postwar Finnish history was the general strike of 1956, a strike of Social Democrat and Communist workers against the high prices caused by the expiry of price control as a result of the refusal of the Rightist members of parliament to sanction any further extension of such controls. Ostensibly the strike was against the employing interest (i.e. the core of the Right), but in fact the chain of events then started also led to antagonism between the workers and the agricultural interest, for agricultural prices rose a second time once the strikers had secured their wage increases, the value of which was thus soon nullified.[9] Both the Social Democratic Party and the trade union movement subsequently split—essentially on the issue of whether it was better to cooperate with the agricultural interest and accept high agricultural subsidies or whether it was better to cooperate with the large industrial employers to promote an economic policy favouring industry rather than agriculture, since the strength of the trade union movement and the Social Democratic Party lay in any case in the urban proletariat and emigration from the countryside was inevitable. In the event, with the heavy devaluation of 1957, it was large-scale industry that won.

The continuing three-cornered conflict situation between workers, agricultural producers, and the industrial interest affected the presidential election of 1961, where in the beginning the orthodox Social Democrats and most of the Conservative-industrial interest supported the candidature of Olavi Honka, a candidate regarded by the Soviet Union as 'Western', so that these internal conflicts took on a foreign-political meaning. Even here, however, the lines were blurred, for Kekkonen received the support of certain leading industrialists, notably Jussi Walden, who, significantly, had large pulp and paper exporting interests to the Soviet Union.[10] In 1968 the lines crossed again and the industrialist interest, including Walden, supported the candidature of the banker Matti Virkkunen, while the Left and Centre, having already come together in the Popular Front government of 1966, were behind Kekkonen. The final triumph of consensus politics, so important, as we have seen, from the standpoint of Finnish foreign policy-makers, came with the continuance in office of President Kekkonen in 1974 by a vote of all the major parties in parliament, including the Conservatives, who have not been in a government since 1966.

Continually breaking through the surface of this consensus, however, is the impact of the underlying three-cornered conflict described above. The feuding between SAK and MTK continues—in a talk given to the University of Turku on 30 January 1973 the then general-secretary of SAK, Niilo Hämäläinen, complained that agriculture was eating up the state budget and that the greater part of agricultural subsidies were paid by taxing the wage-earner. He poured scorn on the regional development policy that has been an important part of the Centre Party programme. In 1974 a somewhat disgruntled deputy-chairman of the Centre Party, Paavo Väyrynen, published a critical study of the Popular Front government of the late 60s and early 70s in which he singled out for attack the Social Democrats' handling of fiscal policy, which, he reasonably argued, had transferred more of the burden of taxation from industry to the shoulders of the average taxpayer. Thus, argued Väyrynen, it was the favouring of industry not agriculture that was responsible for the citizens' increasing tax burdens and the Social Democrats had only themselves to blame.[11] On the other hand when, in the summer of 1974, the Social Democrats wished to impose heavy export levies on the wood, paper and pulp industry, principally paper and pulp—levies that were intended to serve both as an anti-inflationary device and an investment fund—it was the Centre Party that came to the aid of this industry (agriculture and forestry are closely inter-twined) and compelled the government to modify its proposal and allow the wood, paper and pulp industry the chance of channelling back its extra profit into its *own* investment fund.

What, then, is the outcome of this three-cornered conflict? As noted, in internal and external politics the conflict is damped down into a presentation of consensus, but in economic policy the ultimate issue of the conflict is the triumph of big business, who can find their allies alternatively in one camp (the Social Democratic establishment) or in another (the Centre Party), while the traditional political arm of business interests, the Conservative Party, remains out in the cold, though its leading members often simply exercise their power through their business connections and positions.

Throughout the whole of the postwar period the position of these large-scale business interests has been gradually consolidating. Since major industry in Finland tends on the whole not to be particularly labour-intensive, the increasing prosperity that capitalism brought to Finland in the 60s (and according to a TV report of 7 November 1974 Finnish purchasing power rose 60 per cent from 1960 to 1972) has left untouched, among others, the 143,000 Finns who, with the decline of agriculture and the closing of many small industries, were compelled to emigrate to Sweden to find work or employment in place of underemployment (the figure is of net emigration: the total figure, including those who have returned, is well over 200,000). In fairness it should be pointed out that in the spring of 1975 the Finnish research bureau ETLA published findings that indicated that many of those who had left for Sweden in the previous decade were skilled or semi-skilled workers whose motivation in emigrating was less the search for employment than the search for better employment in a period in which there were rising expectations of material well-being.

The Soviet connection

At Yalta Churchill suggested that Finland should on the termination of hostilities be obliged to 'chop down a few trees' as reparations to the Soviet Union.[12] In fact the 12 per cent of its territory Finland had to cede to the Soviet Union by the armistice agreement (see p. 11) meant 12 per cent of its forest resources and 25 per cent of its water-power resources; in consequence it had to resettle over 400,000 people, and pay reparations of $300 million.[13] Though the Soviet Union later reduced this figure by slightly under 25 per cent, the burden of reparations on the Finnish economy was for many years a very heavy one, especially as the Finns were not allowed to pay it off simply by chopping down trees, but had to pay in goods the Soviet Union wanted.[14] This meant rapidly expanding the Finnish shipbuilding industry and doubling the output of the machine industry, though the latter's starting-point was not quite as low as is often asserted since the industry had already expanded significantly during the war.[15] It is, however, undeniable that the stimulating of this branch of industry was of much benefit since it greatly assisted the diversification of Finnish industry.[16] In addition, reparations formed the basis of a renewed trade with the Soviet Union once reparations themselves came to an end in 1952. (In pre-1939 Finland the country's trade with the Soviet Union had fallen to under 1 per cent of the total volume of Finnish foreign trade—it had been approximately 28 per cent in 1913.[17] In 1973 Finnish exports to the Soviet Union formed 11·7 per cent of the whole.)[18]

According to present-day Leftist writers, the reparations period greatly strengthened the capitalist structure of Finland. They argue that the true burden of reparations was in reality paid by the Finnish worker, who suffered low wages throughout this period in the cause of industry that was supposedly making little profit.[19] What happened, however, was that the leading private industries and firms involved received help from the state, and by virtue of their influence in the reparations organ SOTEVA could channel the orders more or less as they desired. In the meantime the most important figures in Finnish commerce and industry saw to it that while trade with the USSR was going to be an acceptable feature of the postwar economic scene, the Russians were certainly not getting any foothold in Finnish industry. In 1947 the head of the Soviet trade delegation P. N. Kumykin pressed hard for the establishment of joint Soviet-Finnish companies (similar to those imposed on the East European countries) throughout the major fields of Finnish industry. In these companies the Soviet Union would have held half the shares, and if the other half had been a Finnish state share this would inevitably have meant a certain Finnish Communist representation among the Finnish directors. Pressure upon the Finnish government from business figures like J. O. Söderhjelm stressed the danger of allowing the country's leading export industries to fall under foreign direction.[20] The Soviet moves were successfully fended off.

This meant not merely the maintenance of the traditional capitalist structure in Finland, but also the keeping open without difficulty of traditional markets in the West. Finland nevertheless entered into a commercial agreement with the Soviet Union in 1947 by which the latter received most-favoured-nation status, and in the same year Finland refused Marshall Aid. The refusal was against the wishes of Finnish industry which desperately needed capital.[21] In this case, in short, Finland's dominant economic interests were not able to make the government dance to their tune. The limitations imposed by the government in terms of national security and the policy that later became crystallized as political neutrality were to override considerations of economic policy. The Finnish government took its cue from the Soviet Union's negative reaction to the Czechs' initial interest in Marshall Aid. This difference in Czech and Finnish behaviour may go some way to explain the difference in the Soviet attitude to the two countries, in the spring of 1948.[22] On the other hand the Fagerholm Social Democrat minority government that was in office from July 1948 to March 1950 was soon accused by the Soviet leaders of wanting to join a 'marshallized Europe'.[23]

The Soviet attitude to Finnish economic policy has two facets. There is first the strictly economic side. Finnish reparation goods, for example, were highly valued by the Soviet Union in the reconstruction period because of the fine standards of Finnish workmanship. But secondly the Soviet leaders have a strong interest in preventing Finland from participating in the political-economic expansion of Western Europe. This aspect may be seen to be in essence political. In fine, Finland must continue to be a neutral borderland—in regard to EEC just as much as in regard to NATO. What Soviet-Finnish economic relations show, however, is the interaction of the economic and political aspects.

Since a large part of the economy in Finland, and more particularly the metal industry, depends greatly on Soviet orders, there have been occasions when the Soviet Union, in pursuit of an essentially political objective, has suspended orders. This it did, together with non-implementation of a promised loan, in the 'night-frost crisis' of 1958 during the third Fagerholm government. That government, as we have seen, broke up. It might well be that the use of an economic weapon in this instance was some kind of reminder to the Finns not to indulge in wishful thinking about tying up with Western European economic integration (a political matter, of course, for the Russians) since the Rome Treaty had been signed only a few months before.[24] The wider problem of Germany (with which the emergence of the EEC connects) has already been dealt with in chapter 2.

Conversely the Soviet authorities have also been able to use their political position for economic ends. The most obvious case of this was the contract for the building of the Loviisa nuclear power station in southern Finland. A preliminary understanding with the British had been arrived at in this matter after the tender had been open for international competition, but the decision was then reversed and the contract awarded to the Soviet Union, with whom Finland has a Treaty of Friendship, Cooperation and Mutual Assistance. But this matter is by no means as straightforward as it seems. One official explanation put out by the Finns is that by doing a deal with the Soviet Union Finland saves on foreign currency and can adjust its balance of payments more satisfactorily, for the nature of Finnish-Soviet trade is that it is undertaken in barter terms in trade agreements planned for a five-year period, so that a deficit in one year can be adjusted the next. And for the total five-year period goods are matched by goods. Further, it was a fact that at the end of the 60s the Finns had difficulty in securing sufficient imports from the Soviet Union to balance the volume of goods they were willing to export. The Loviisa contract, as well as the ordering of new locomotives from the Soviet Union which Finnish industry would equally well have been able to supply, eased this import problem.

Caution should also be used in interpreting the Soviet action in raising in the autumn of 1973 the price of oil exported to Finland to the Rotterdam notation level. It is true that until this point many Finns had been congratulating their country on having escaped the worst effects of the oil crisis by virtue of the trade agreements with the Soviet Union, for in these agreements the price, payable by bartered goods from Finland, was fixed beforehand. The Soviet authorities nevertheless demanded an adjustment when the price rose elsewhere. This was in line with the Soviet Union's general trade policy towards non-Comecon countries in recent years, namely to demand the maximum price achievable on the world market, and, characteristically, the price of Soviet oil to the Comecon countries themselves was raised a little over a year later. When the Soviet authorities raised the price of oil to Finland, the Finns were importing 74 per cent of their requirements from the Soviet Union, and at the opening session of the Finnish parliament in 1974 the president gave the somewhat exaggerated figure of 5 per cent as the amount of extra drag on GNP caused by the burden of new oil prices. In the meantime the foreign minister, Karjalainen, had already taken a pro-Soviet line. He explained to the Finnish people that as a matter of fact it had already been agreed between Finland and the Soviet Union in the 1950s that world market prices would be followed in the trade agreements between the two countries. Karjalainen went on to add that while the situation was now unfavourable for Finland, it would in the long run turn out to be favourable, as long as the Finns too kept their own exports to the

Soviet Union up to world market-prices.[25] Others in Finland were inclined to see the benefits for Finland accruing basically from the increased production—and therefore employment prospects—that paying for the dearer oil entailed. Since trade with the Soviet Union is barter trade, the oil must be paid for by increased exports to the USSR, and this will mean an expansion in the Finnish metal and textile industries and further orders for the 'new export' of more commercially sensitive products such as furniture. Sections of the metal industry, the whole of the textile industry and most of the 'new export' are labour-intensive industries.

The long-term benefits for Finland were thus clear. On the other hand it was suggested in business circles that the Finnish state oil refining monopoly's negotiators had been clumsy in their negotiations with their Soviet opposite numbers.[26] Since there is reason to believe that oil from the Middle East was selling in Western Europe in 1974 for over $14 a barrel, it is difficult to envisage what other course of action the Finnish negotiators could have followed.

It would be easy to jump to swift conclusions about the role of Soviet trade within the wider context of Finnish-Soviet relations. The Soviet Union has estimated that it could supply 37 per cent of Finland's electricity needs and Technopromexport, the Soviet agency that built the Loviisa nuclear power station, was to begin negotiations with the Finnish authorities for another nuclear power station (1,000 megawatts) in 1976.[27] The Soviet authorities have said that they will guarantee the fuel for this. A Soviet-Finnish natural gas pipeline has already been opened. Does all this mean that Finnish security is inevitably being weakened by a growing dependence on the Soviet Union for the basic supply of energy?[28]

In a conflict situation between East and West it is difficult to imagine how Finland could protect any possible alternative energy supply from other sources. The Finns have recently entertained a top-level Saudi Arabian trade delegation in their country (about 10 per cent of Finnish oil imports currently come from Saudi Arabia), but import by tanker through the Baltic would be a highly vulnerable source of supply in wartime. Equally important, however, is the question of the extent to which the Soviet Union might be able to manipulate Finnish foreign policy through Finland's energy dependence on it. The possibility is under certain circumstances envisageable, though as far as imports of Soviet oil are concerned, it rather looks as if the Soviet Union will be unable even to supply all Comecon's requirements by the 1980s, so that Finland's chances of getting oil from USSR are likely to diminish, perhaps considerably. Anyway the Finnish answer to energy dependence is to pursue the lines of policy that have been described hitherto in this work—the building-up of international, multilateral structures for cooperation. This policy depends for its fulfilment upon an effective and firm response from the West, a series of reasoned and reasonable rejoinders to the Soviet détente proposals.

In effect this is a question of building long-term structures. More and more Finland's external policy must concern itself with short-term pressing problems, often of an economic nature. The oil crisis hit Finland badly so that the Finnish consumer is paying for what has been estimated to be the dearest petrol in Europe—Finnish petrol is much dearer than Swedish (Sweden imports 75 per cent of its oil from Western companies).[29] It has been argued that the Finnish government has not done all it could to ensure alternative oil supplies from non-Soviet sources. Indeed, the government would actually like to increase the import of crude from the Soviet Union and refine more in Finland, which might turn out to be a somewhat cheaper way of dealing with the problem, but the Soviet Union claims to be unable to supply any more. Broadly the Finnish government justifies its dealings with the Soviet government from the point of view of the saving in foreign exchange that occurs when Finland can pay for its oil imports by a gradually-adjusted increase in the export of goods. The junior minister of finance, Esko Niskanen, has even gone so far as to say that trade with the Soviet Union has saved the Finnish economy.[30] The Conservative newspaper *Uusi Suomi*, in an editorial of 2 February 1974, admitted likewise that the bilateral trade with the Soviet Union was undoubtedly advantageous to the Finns under present circumstances.

These circumstances are that Finland's exports to the West are running into growing difficulties, especially many of the products of the staple exporting industry of paper, pulp, and wood, while at the same time imports from the West show a disturbing tendency to surge upwards. As reported in the *Helsingin Sanomat* of 23 June 1975, *Pravda*'s Helsinki correspondent was ready to point out that through Finland's free-trade agreement with the EEC the country had been dragged ever deeper into the general crisis afflicting the capitalist world. It is certainly true that the trade deficit with the EEC is the greatest that Finland has. And it can equally well be said that if Finland did not have the advantage of Soviet imports (which, it must be repeated, do not produce a balance-of-payments problem, owing to the bilateral barter nature of Finnish-Soviet trade), and if Finland had instead to import a corresponding amount from the West, the situation would be near-catastrophic.

Trade with the Soviet Union is also very much an employment question. On 27 February 1974 it was decided to treble the amount of ready-made clothing to be exported to the USSR. The export of machinery and other equipment will rise by one-third. In addition the Finns will continue to build industrial and mining complexes on Soviet soil. This work has so far been mainly in the border-areas, e.g. at Svetogorsk (formerly the Finnish district of Ensio) the Finns have constructed a large paper and pulp factory-complex, while further north at Kostamus they have built a mining centre. In future they may even take part in comparable projects at Norilsk, Siberia, and it has been suggested that joint Russo-Finnish concerns might build electric power stations in third countries. The value of such projects for the Finnish labour-market is considerable. One of the leading officials of the Kainuu district in north-eastern Finland has estimated that the building of Kostamus is a 'condition of life' for the Kainuu district,[31] where previously unemployment and underemployment have been endemic. In certain areas projects of this kind have done more for local development than Finland's own development area policy.

This would seem to be a far cry from the days when Söderhjelm prevented the formation of joint Soviet-Finnish industrial enterprise, though admittedly what was then at stake was the prospect of Soviet enterprise in Finland and not the reverse situation.

The Western connection

But Söderhjelm was mainly concerned to keep Finland's trade with the West open and this goal has not been abandoned, either by Finnish industry or the Finnish government. Indeed, apart from the important ideological aspects of this question, this is otherwise a perfectly natural objective, for since the Soviet Union itself tends to produce the same type of forest-industry products as the Finns, there is an obvious difficulty in tying Finland's export trade—in which the products of the wood, paper and pulp industry form even now more than half and in 1950 formed 85 per cent[32]—too closely to the Soviet Union. As far as reparations were concerned, the share of the wood, paper and pulp industry (less than one-third) was already paid off by the end of 1948.[33]

In fact, however, one of the earliest problems that drew Finnish government and business interests towards contact with the West in the immediate post-armistice period was not the question of re-opening markets but that of obtaining credits and capital with which to furnish some of the basic raw materials (e.g. sheet-steel) and equipment for the reparations industries. Both Sweden and the United States were helpful in this respect. In the years up to 1952 the Americans granted more than $150 million in credits to Finland, even though Finland did not get Marshall Aid.[34] A major concern of the Finns at the time that the 1948 Treaty was being negotiated was to ensure that these credits would not dry up because of the treaty; the US Export-Import Bank loans were especially important then both for the reparation exports and for exports to the West, and Finnish diplomats and politicians tried hard to convince the Americans that Finland had not been Sovietized by the treaty.[35]

They succeeded. Between 1955 and 1962 the Finns received from the World Bank loans to the value of $114 million both for the development of the wood, paper and pulp industry and for the construction of power-stations.[36] But by this time the import of capital from the West, though undoubtedly an important factor, had been none the less superseded in importance by the need to ensure widening participation in markets abroad, primarily in the West. The gradual freeing of world trade through GATT was a desirable objective from the Finnish viewpoint. In the introductory pages of this chapter reference has already been made to some of the measures taken during these years to help the Finnish export industry. However, one of the most significant steps towards closer economic contacts with the West was the drawing up of the protocol of the 'Helsinki Club', as it was called, which was then signed between Finland and the OEEC countries in 1957, considerably easing the payments position in the trade between Finland and these countries. It was Finland's own special equivalent to OEEC's European Payments Union, and the matter was arranged in this way because OEEC was a follow-up of the Marshall Plan, and in consequence Finland was not a member. The protocol was renewed yearly till 1968, when Finland was able to join the reconstituted organization known as OECD.[37] Finland had by this time for many years had observer status in the OEEC's pulp and paper committee. So active was Söderhjelm in that committee that he had once been proposed for its chairman.[38]

By advancing in partial stages the Finns have been able to avoid too marked and obvious a participation in forms of Western European economic integration while at the same time they have been able to keep their markets open. A delicate situation already began to develop in 1956 when the discussions within OEEC were started that led to the Treaty of Rome of 1957. Apart from taking the measures described above, the obvious counter-weight from the Finnish point of view was a regional form of economic cooperation that would be somewhat distinct from the emerging EEC. This could only mean some kind of formalized Nordic economic cooperation.

The framework for such cooperation was afforded by the existence of the Nordic Council, a consultative body, to which the five Northern European countries of Denmark, Norway, Iceland, Sweden, and Finland all belonged. The Finns in fact did not begin to participate in the work of the Council till 1956, and only then on condition that military and security policy matters were not to be discussed there, a condition that protected their neutrality and, indirectly, the interests of the Soviet Union. When the Council had first started functioning in 1953 the Soviet Union had been hostile to it and Finland had initially not joined it,[39] only doing so after the renewal of the 1948 Treaty in 1955 and the return of Porkkala. Nevertheless Finland had already signed the Common Labour Market Treaty with other Nordic Council members in July 1954. This was of tremendous significance for the Finns, for it enabled them to export their surplus population to Sweden, where, without the need for work-permits, they readily found employment, being the largest immigrant population from one Nordic country to another. It may be said without exaggeration that for Finland, a small country with a large-scale capital-intensive industry geared to export, for many years the greatest importance of Nordic cooperation was the opportunity it afforded to export Finns. Within the last two or three years, however, more Finns have returned from Sweden than have emigrated there, but the net loss has been of the nature of something like 250,000–300,000 in the period 1946–72, and in recent months a net loss has again begun to occur.

This internal pressure for North European economic cooperation (due in part to the inability of Finnish industry and the needs of Swedish industry to absorb the people displaced from a slowly-declining Finnish agriculture)[40] was complemented by the impact of external forces that in part spurred on such cooperation and in part set the limits to it. In 1956, under the leadership of the Swedish official Nils Montan, the joint Swedish, Norwegian, and Finnish delegations to the GATT conference of that year successfully cooperated to secure reductions in the tariffs on pulp and paper in the face of the reluctance and opposition of Britain, West Germany, and the Benelux countries.[41] This seemed to be indicative of the scope for North European economic cooperation that had been fitfully promoted since 1948 by a joint North European commission of economic cooperation (with which Finland was not, however, associated till 1956). In 1957 the North European trade and industrial associations began to consult together about a Nordic Customs Union, and this project became the major topic for the Nordic Council. It was advantageous to the Finns for several reasons. The GATT rules allowed for regional economic associations and the tariff reductions occurring would be a continuation, however partial, of GATT's work. Further, since only 8 per cent of Finland's imports came from the goods scheduled in the project for liberalization, the branch of Finnish industry that worked for the home market would not be greatly affected.[42] On the other hand the Nordic countries, producing similar goods to the Finns, were not expected to take a large share of Finnish exports either. Participation in a North European customs agreement was therefore at this stage expected to be a beneficial but limited step forward for the Finnish economy.

When, however, the impact of the formation of the Outer Seven economic grouping made itself felt in Northern Europe, and Swedish business interests and government began at once to urge the advantages of a widened liberalized market area, a certain petulant tone crept into the statements of the Finnish representatives that was not altogether genuine, for there were obvious advantages for the Finns in entering a widened free-trade area, to which so many of their exports—in the case of the United Kingdom, for example—were directed.[43] Finland, it was claimed, now had on grounds of economic necessity to join in the negotiations with the Outer Seven, otherwise the position of its main exports (i.e. the products of wood, paper and pulp industry) would be damaged, say, on the UK market, by competition from the Swedes.[44]

We have seen how the FINEFTA agreement, which was signed on 27 March 1961, strengthened Finland's orientation to Western markets. The power of EFTA in this case is all the more remarkable if two considerations are borne in mind. In the first place, as noted earlier, one of the most astonishing characteristics of the trading relations developed under FINEFTA was the rapid growth of Finnish-Swedish trade, itself a consequence of and stimulus to diversification in the Finnish export pattern. Yet the projected Nordic Customs Union had never been envisaged as producing anything of this magnitude in inter-Nordic trade. In the second place it should be noted that the EFTA countries themselves did not make any real effort to get Finland into an association with EFTA. Indeed, some initial reservations were voiced from the EFTA side. It was suggested that the most-favoured-nation position retained by the Soviet Union in Finnish trade might lead indirectly to the penetration of EFTA markets by the Soviet trade agencies.[45] Or again it was feared that the creation of a special status for Finland might lead to a demand for a special status for, say, Austria. In this way EFTA's structure might be weakened, the argument ran.[46] It was thus from the Finnish rather than from the EFTA side that the impetus came for the association of Finland with the EFTA states. One British diplomat described Finnish industry as 'mad keen for Finland to associate with EFTA, foreseeing terrible handicaps, indeed disaster, if it did not'. The force of the attraction that EFTA exerted for Finland's dominant business interests, the role that EFTA had previously played in upsetting plans for strictly North European economic arrangements, and the subsequent success of EFTA in stimulating North European trade nevertheless, proved the point later to be made by Amitai Etzioni that economically as well as politically Northern Europe is too weak an area to form a cohesive and distinct unit.[47]

The advantages of the FINEFTA agreement were obvious to the most superficial observer. Finnish exports now entered with ease a market area of 100 million people (the North European market area would have been restricted to under 20 million people). On the other hand, apart from retaining their special trading relationship with the Soviet Union, the Finns won other privileges under their agreement with EFTA. Agriculture, which could hardly have withstood foreign competition, remained entirely outside the agreement. And in regard to some of Finland's more vulnerable industrial products, such as textiles, ceramics, and certain metal goods, tariff reductions were to take place at so slow a rate that the last tariffs were not to be removed till 1 January 1970.

In justifying the FINEFTA agreement, the banker Reino Rossi went on to argue that the question was not merely one of economic necessity but should also be seen in the light of the impossibility of

raising living standards if Finland decided to withdraw behind a
high tariff-wall into a kind of economic autarky.[48] These two viewpoints are fundamentally contradictory. Was EFTA compelling or
was it alluring? Rossi's statement seems to indicate that there was
after all an alternative to EFTA, namely a greater degree of protection for home industries. The enormous export of surplus
Finnish labour-power (human beings) to Sweden in the 1960s was a
mute and melancholy witness to the ghost of the alternative. By the
end of the 60s leading SAK officials were arguing that EFTA had
been a 'bad deal' that brought in goods and took out people.[49] The
more sophisticated analyses of academic critics not themselves
opposed to integration as such, tended to argue that the benefits to
Finland's exports had been exaggerated, for the strong position of
products of the wood, paper and pulp industry on the world
market would anyway have furnished them with sufficient outlets.[50]
Professor Veikko Reinikainen of the Turku School of Economics
argued at the end of the 60s, in Finland's leading business journal,
that Finland's recent export figures (representing, he claimed, more
trade diversion and less trade creation than the EFTA secretariat in
Geneva was prepared to admit) were an inadequate criterion by
which to judge the EFTA connection. Finland had shown in-
sufficient 'transformation ability' to adapt itself to the uneven
effects of this measure of integration. 'Profit' should not be the only
criterion, but greater use should have been made of industrial
subsidies and regional development policy to prevent the unemployment that drove so many to look for work abroad or in the
south of Finland, where housing and environmental problems were
acute.[51]

   In general, critics of EFTA have stressed the government's
ignoring of the problem of excessive imports and the attendant
balance-of-payments difficulties (that led to the devaluation of 1967)
and the unwillingness of Finland's ruling groups to admit the
restrictions on economic policy that both EFTA and GATT have
brought, for a policy of curbing imports is contrary to the rules of
both organizations.[52] This little-recognized fact is a pointer to the
fundamental truth that West European integration—just as the
Soviet connection—exacts its price and imposes its limitations on
Finland.

   When EFTA's future began to seem uncertain with the re-
doubled attempt of Britain to enter the EEC, a general consensus
arose in Finland to try once more the prospect of a North European

economic arrangement. The fate of the latter project, Nordek, is an apt illustration of the pressures of external forces upon North European economic cooperation. The Nordek project, which had the blessing of EFTA, was to consist not merely of a customs union but certain common institutions, notably a central investment bank, were also to be created[53] (the importance of the latter idea for Northern Europe may be seen in the continuing interest, in spite of the failure of Nordek, in the foundation of such a bank).[54] This was particularly desired by the Finns. One of the supposed advantages of the Nordic Customs Union planned in the late 50s had been the projected investment bank that went with it,[55] and Article 19 of the Helsinki Treaty of Northern European Cooperation, signed in 1962, had stressed the need for a common investment policy, but little was done thereafter.[56] By the late 60s, however, the Finns were actively trying to get Swedish investment to Finland (the most successful example being the foundation of the Saab-Valmet works at Uusikaupunki by joint private Swedish and Finnish government enterprise).[57] For the Finns a Nordic investment bank would be a means of channelling Swedish capital to Finland, a solution greatly favoured by the Social Democratic Party, which had strong reservations otherwise about international capital movements, multinational corporations, etc. Opinion in Finland generally supported Nordek as a manageable form of integration, for it did not simply mean a lowering of tariff barriers still further, but involved too compensatory forms of cooperative endeavour such as capital and technical information flows.[58]

In other Nordic countries, however, the situation was more complex. For several years there had been a growing cooperation between the Nordic countries in, for example, the Kennedy Round of tariff negotiations, but while approving of this type of economic cooperation, the Danish industrialists did not want to take the further step of a Nordic customs union.[59] Even the supporters of Nordek seemed inclined to argue in terms of its existence as a transitional organization. The prime ministers of the Nordic countries seem to have agreed to set Nordek on a course that would follow the EEC's development, and even to have regarded Nordek as some kind of 'training ground' for future alignment or linking with a widened European community.[60] One of the clearest expressions of this viewpoint was given by Max Jakobson in an interview with Robert Eastbrook on New York TV. When Eastbrook cast doubts upon a future Finnish entry to EEC, and grounded his doubts on the probable reaction of the Soviet Union, Jakobson jumped in with a denial that the question depended on the Soviet Union at all and told his interviewer that no Scandinavian country would go alone into the EEC but that 'we are uniting our strength now [i.e. Nordek] in order to be firm when the moment arrives'.[61]

Jakobson was wrong. The Hague Conference held in the late autumn of 1969 which extended an invitation to a widened membership of the Community had an attraction for both the Danes and the Norwegians, but frightened the Finns. The Finns called off a meeting planned to discuss Nordek in Turku in December, and on 12 January 1970 the Finnish government announced that if any Northern country began to take steps to enter into membership of a European economic association while the Nordek negotiations were taking place, Finland would reserve the right to suspend its own participation in the Nordek project. As time went on the Finns became increasingly hesitant. Differences of opinion arose between the Social Democratic prime minister, Mauno Koivisto, who was more enthusiastic for Nordek, and the more cautious foreign minister, Ahti Karjalainen. But both began to stress that for the Finns Nordek was not a means to a wider integration: they both emphasized Finnish neutrality and the importance of the trading link with the Soviet Union. On 24 March the Finnish cabinet made a declaration to the effect that it did not intend at that moment in time to sign the Nordek agreement.

It is still difficult to ascertain and evaluate all the factors involved in the break-up of the Nordek project. One explanation is to see that, through the weak-point of Denmark,[62] the EEC, whose power had been recognized from the start by the Nordek negotiators, disturbed the project, and an important element in this disturbance was that the Finns took fright at the too swift conjuring up of the EEC presence. They feared for the image of their neutrality and they feared the confirmation of the distrust of the Soviet Union in the project. The Soviet government had not liked the plans for a Nordic Customs Union proposed ten years earlier[63] and their commentators made no secret of their suspicions of Nordek,[64] even if the Soviet government did not officially openly proclaim its hostility to the project. Now, it seemed, the Soviet authorities had been right in their suspicions that West European integration plans included attempts to take in Northern Europe.

But there are other explanations. A Finnish Leftist viewpoint sees the real reason for Finland's hesitancy and withdrawal neither in the fear of a tarnished neutrality nor in the fear of Soviet reactions. The explanation put forward is that Finnish industrial and commercial circles, realizing that the EEC was interested in Northern Europe, saw that Finland had a chance to get a free-trade agreement of its own with the EEC. This agreement, in spite of requiring an initial period of maintaining tariffs on certain goods, would be a surer way for Finnish exports to the EEC markets than anything Nordek could provide. The Centre Party foreign minister Karjalainen, as an old-time Agrarian close to the wood-working interests, is held to have been influenced by this outlook.[65]

On 6 April 1970 the Finns began negotiations with EEC, describing them in contrast to the Nordic negotiations as 'defensive'. The essentials of the pattern that had first appeared in the late 50s had now been repeated. The *primus motor* was Western European economic integration, but the *secundus motor* as far as changing Finland's position was concerned was Britain. Britain through EFTA upset the plans for a Nordic Customs Union at the end of the 50s, and at the end of the 60s British action caused the shrinking of EFTA while the Danish fear of difficulties with British trade was at least one important factor in the failure of the Nordek alternative to materialize. In turn the Finns' fear of losing UK markets was explained as being an important factor both in the FINEFTA agreement and Finland's free-trade agreement with the enlarged EEC, with Britain now a member of it. The pressure of this force, i.e. the indirect effect upon Finland of the consequences of British policy elsewhere, is of a different kind from the suspicions expressed by the Soviet Union towards Finland's growing relationship with West European integration. Nevertheless the indirect effect of British actions upon determining Finnish policy has far more importance than the constraints on that policy that may arise as a result of Finnish susceptibilities to what the Russians might think.

The Finnish negotiators stressed all along that Finland was only seeking a free-trade agreement with EEC—i.e. once again simply seeking to protect its exports—and that there was no question of any further integration. The very vocal opposition to a connection with the EEC that did arise in Finland argued its case, however, very often in terms of Finland's being drawn inevitably into the EEC sphere. Indeed, even in 1961, there was clear evidence that some members of the right wing of the Social Democratic Party and banking circles were in favour of an economic arrangement with EEC precisely to facilitate the import of capital from Western

Europe.[66] By 1969 sceptical observers were pointing out that but for Finland's foreign policy considerations the country would join EEC.[67] By the early 1970s banking circles were showing an open interest in the provision of capital as a result of an EEC connection.[68] A broader statement of 'economic realism' was made on 11 September 1973 by Päiviö Hetemäki, a leading Finnish industrialist and member of the Bank of Finland, who said that Finland could not but adapt itself to the economic trends set by the big states, and that if the government did not see to it that this adaptation occurred, the Bank of Finland would.

The attraction of the EEC for dominant Finnish economic interests was therefore clear. The Finnish government's attitude was more cautious. They argued openly enough for a realization of the fact that the nature of Finland's economy (with more than 70 per cent of its exports directed to the West) and *the pattern laid down by GATT and EFTA* necessitated a continuance of the same trend of development by an arrangement with the EEC.[69] In short, the pattern laid down previously by the dominant economic forces was the one to follow. On the other hand the government endeavoured to satisfy dissident or potentially dissident interests in two ways. First, agricultural products were outside the agreement—this meant that the Centre Party would inevitably support it, while within the agreement protection for certain sensitive products was to be given in the form of transition periods of eight to twelve years before the final, full reduction of tariffs. Quite outside the agreement the government ultimately secured the passing of a number of 'protection laws' which enabled it, among other things, to impose export levies, if necessary on flourishing exports, for the benefit of the rest of industry. What happened when the government tried to impose these levies on the pulp and paper industry in the summer of 1974 has already been described.

Economically speaking it is difficult to see from the EEC side any great interest or pressure upon Finland (as distinct from the undoubted interest the EEC had in Northern Europe as a whole)—the Finnish market of under 5 millions is anyway small. The EEC's political motivation may have been more important, but at the time of writing evidence is lacking. As far as the import of capital is concerned, the interest again would rather seem to come from the Finnish side,[70] where the Commission for Foreign Investments and the Bank of Finland issue booklets with titles like *Establishing a Business in Finland* and *Financial Markets in Finland*. Throughout

1974 government spokesmen have stressed the need to encourage further foreign loans to cover the enormous costs of building new nuclear power-stations.[71] At a lower investment level the towns of Pori and Espoo (the latter through the part-mediation of the Workers' Savings Bank) have sought foreign loans (in the case of Espoo a dollar loan) for building and energy projects.[72] On the other hand the minister for foreign trade, Jermu Laine, has warned that the continual financing of the trade deficit by the taking of foreign loans may well lead in a few years time to a situation in which Finland's foreign debt will reach a total of 20 per cent of GNP. Laine pointed to the significant fact that the share of this kind of indebtedness had risen during the EFTA period from 4 to 12 per cent of GNP. His conclusion was that Finland should export more and demand a higher price for its exports.[73]

Thus on all sides the dominance of Finland's great exporting interests is confirmed. Somewhat ironically the most important of these, the pulp and paper industry, will suffer most from the tariffs still in force temporarily under the EEC free-trade agreement, for while pulp and newsprint will be tariff-free, the Community duties on imports of fine paper and most related products from Finland will not be abolished till 1 January 1984. This significant fact is revealing from more than one angle. It is, for one thing, clear evidence that there are interests within the EEC area, namely its own paper industry, that fear rather than welcome Finland's connection with the EEC. Indeed, the English paper manufacturers pressured their own government, when Britain left EFTA, for the EEC to insist on the higher EEC tariff for Finnish imported paper to Britain. From another point of view, however, the fact that the Finnish pulp and paper industry can endure these tariffs for so long a transitional period testifies at one and the same time to the power of the industry[74]—it can triumph over this initial obstacle—and to the strangeness therefore of the industry's insistence at all on a free-trade agreement with the EEC—as the Communist paper *Kansan Uutiset* pointed out in an important editorial of 7 June 1972. The answer of the industry to the charge that from its point of view a free-trade agreement with the EEC was unnecessary has been to argue that by accepting long transitional duties on its products it made way for a compromise solution that gave easier access in the near future to the products of other Finnish industries on the EEC markets or,[75] equally important, enabled Finland in turn to seek a longer period of protection for some of its own more vulnerable industries. Broadly speaking, however, it may be assumed that what has been at issue has been Finnish industry's feeling that it can face the long-term challenge of wider markets and can endure the limitations imposed by the EEC agreement, which include, among others, a prohibition on export bounties even for firms in the development areas.

And so in any case Finland, through the impact of its more prominent economic interests, supported, it must be said, by the Centre Party and most of the Social Democratic Party (an important minority of Social Democratic dissidents agreed with the Communist opposition to the EEC agreement), and by all the bourgeois parties finally adopted an agreement that bound its economy closer than before to Western European economic integration. An interesting play upon the term 'neutrality' now came into question. The leader of the Swedish People's Party in Finland, Professor Jan-Magnus Jansson, a minister in the government, argued in a speech of 31 May 1973 that if Finland did not enter into a free-trade agreement with EEC its neutrality would automatically be suspect. Instead therefore of political neutrality guaranteeing economic arrangements with all sides, the opportunity to make economic choices became a criterion of political neutrality.

But neutrality, according to the Finns' own estimation, rests much upon its credibility in the eyes of the beholder. What would the Soviet Union think?

The free-trade agreement with the EEC had actually been initialled by the Finns as early as 21 July 1972 (though it was not ratified till 1973). On 19 July 1972 the minority Social Democratic government resigned, claiming that only a government with the backing of the majority of the Finnish parliament could afford to sign the agreement. Of some significance for the Social Democrats was the fear that if they tried to introduce the EEC agreement alone it would damage their credibility with the Soviet Union. On 4 September a reconstituted majority government came into office in which the Social Democrats shared the main burden with the Centre Party. The slow manœuvring could now begin that would contain the internal opposition to EEC (the dissident Social Democrats and SKDL).

Meanwhile President Kekkonen, at the end of August, had visited Leonid Brezhnev at the latter's dacha at Zavidovo and there, together with Alexei Kosygin, they had discussed the vexed topic of Finland's free trade agreement with the EEC. The Soviet leaders had hitherto not officially committed themselves on this question and at Zavidovo they stressed that it was Finland's own affair. They nevertheless expressed to Kekkonen their concern lest friendship between Finland and the Soviet Union be impaired by the EEC agreement and indicated that in their view the objective of the EEC was a political encroachment, an opinion that, considering the slender evidence of economic advantages for the EEC in the deal, is hardly one to be rejected out of hand. Kekkonen's response was to give a personal assurance that the course of Finnish-Soviet relations would not be changed. This, in effect, would seem to have committed him to becoming president again, though as a consequence of the revelations of the Zavidovo talks by the Swedish journalist Tor Högnäs, in the *Dagens Nyheter* of 31 October 1972, a scandal blew up in Finland concerning leaks to the press, and at one point a petulant Kekkonen said he did not wish to be president. His ruffled pride soothed, he nevertheless agreed to continue in office (if there were no popular presidential election) and the whole outcome of the Zavidovo incident may be said to have been of the nature of a triumph for the dominant economic interests in Finland. After all, it would have been very difficult for the Soviet Union to have pressured Finland not to sign the free-trade agreement with the EEC at a time when the Finns were pushing so hard for the Security Conference. The cards in Finnish-Soviet relations were thus stacked at this point of time in favour of the Finns.

It is true that the Finns found it expedient, as noted, to enter into an agreement with Comecon, being the first West European market-economy country to do so. This possibility had been open to the Finns since 1959, when the Comecon rules were changed, but the Finns were then wary of becoming too closely associated with Comecon. Only when the chance arose of securing extended economic relations with the Soviet bloc without damaging Western trade but, on the contrary, balancing it (politically too), did the Finns make an agreement with Comecon. This was followed by individual agreements on tariffs with certain East European countries, the KEVSOS agreements, as they are called: in 1974 agreements of this kind were made with Bulgaria and Hungary and in 1975 with Czechoslovakia and East Germany. But here again the same dangers are evident for the weaker Finnish industries serving only the home market as are evident in any trade agreement with the Western economic integration organizations—as, indeed, Reinikainen pointed out there would be. A Finnish trade journal has already complained of the sale of East German household electrical appliances at knock-down prices.[76]

But the major Finnish export industries need not let this concern them, while politically speaking the Finnish government in turn is inclined to view the KEVSOS agreements as a triumph of Finnish neutrality. The actual agreements are modelled on Finland's free-trade agreement with the EEC—itself a clever piece of manipulation—and the Finns have gone on to offer their KEVSOS agreements as a model that the EEC might bear in mind when the different EEC states negotiate—as they could do in theory up to 1 January 1975, and in practice perhaps for longer—bilateral trade agreements with Comecon countries. These matters the Finns also wanted to bring out in the discussions on the contents of the second basket of the Security Conference.[77]

In theory the high point of Finnish neutrality has surely been reached. A proud editorial in the newspaper *Turun Sanomat* on 20 February 1973 pointed out that Finnish neutrality required the establishment of relations with both economic blocs and that in this way Finland would serve in its role of bridge-builder between East and West. The latter viewpoint reflected the trappings of the official presentation of Finnish foreign policy. Seen more realistically, however, Finland's position in a Europe with increasing integration projects is to ensure that it is not, in the first place, cut out from what the Finns call 'the international division of labour'.

In the second place, in entering into a variety of relationships with the various economic forces in Europe the Finns must ensure that they are not swamped by them. 'The international division of labour' exacts its own obvious price in the failure of the weaker Finnish industries to survive the competition that participation in integration projects brings. The sensitivity of Finnish leaders to the charge of having their economic policy directed from outside may be seen in the remark made by the minister of foreign trade, Jermu Laine, on 7 June 1973 in the course of a discussion in the OECD Council of Ministers in Paris.[78] Laine praised the value for Finland of OECD's research on the effects of environmental policy on the workings of the paper and pulp industry, but made a general reservation against the inevitable acceptance of the OECD's economic and social policy's goals as guidelines for the member states. In particular, as far as the EEC itself is concerned, the Finns continually stress that in their free-trade agreement there is no 'development paragraph' that would anticipate closer forms of economic integration in the future. The direction of Finnish policy is thus to remain in Finnish hands.

But the indirect impact of external forces on the formation of Finnish policy is necessarily great—the consequences for Finland of the changes in British policy have already been mentioned. The impact of these external forces is nevertheless cushioned and to some extent even hidden by virtue of the fact that in Finland there are diverse political, social, and economic groupings, some of which (like the trading interest and a large part of the professional class) are pro-Western in outlook, others (like the SKDL supporters) are sympathetic to the Soviet Union, while yet others (such as the younger generation in the Social Democratic Party) are inclined to look with favour on elements from both systems. Then there are the supporters of expediency in the Centre Party.

The existence of these internal forces—the pattern that supports the external policy of neutrality, which is the characterization given to Finland's independence from political blocs—fosters the Finns' belief that they themselves make their own choice as to the economic arrangements they have with the outside world. In fact once having made certain choices—in regard to GATT, EFTA, the EEC, or in regard to receiving the bulk of their energy supplies from the Soviet Union—the Finns, like any other Western nation, become bound by the harsh dictates of international trade.

With an inflation that was running in the summer of 1975 at 18 per cent, with a foreign trade deficit that by May 1975 was double that of the corresponding period of the previous year,[79] the Finnish government was trying to stem the country's ever mounting imbalance of payments by an import deposit system. The Import Deposit Act, which had come into force on 24 March 1975, and was possibly inspired by comparable measures taken in Italy to deal with its chronic trade deficit, empowered the government to levy a deposit of up to 30 per cent on a large class of imports for a period of up to six months during which no interest was payable on the deposit. Roughly 63 per cent of imports have been subjected to the import deposit system and the average deposit rate has been about 20 per cent.[80] The creation of a system of this kind obviates the necessity for import controls and prohibitions that would be offensive to Finland's GATT, EFTA, and EEC obligations. But import deposits have not been liked by Finland's Western trading partners either—the EFTA countries already protested about them in the spring of 1975.

However, the bond that tied Finland to the Western economic system and its demands tightened most obviously in June. Unable any longer to handle their balance-of-payments problem without a foreign loan, the Finns received a loan of 735 million Finmarks from the International Monetary Fund. There were conditions attached to it. Finland had to dismantle its import deposit system as soon as possible (it had been scheduled to run till 23 March 1976) and had to pursue a tight money policy that would inevitably mean further cuts in consumption and public expenditure (prior to the securing of this loan Sorsa's government had already made cuts in certain public sectors, for example, education, evidently with the intention of making, *inter alia*, a favourable impression upon the IMF). These conditions bind future governments. The existence of obligations of this kind upon Finland should be remembered when *Finnlandisierung* is discussed. It was with pardonable exaggeration that a commentator in the newspaper *Ilta Sanomat* wrote on 10 June 1975, with reference to the conditions imposed upon his country's economic policy by the IMF, that they make trade union leaders, parliaments and even governments seem somewhat superfluous. Seppo Ahti's comment is an exaggeration of the popular press. It is not without significance, however, that it is the Bank of Finland that serves as the enforcement agency of these conditions and that it was the Bank's director, Mauno Koivisto, who informed future governments that they are bound by them.

Notes

1. These figures are given by H. Luukkanen in *Kansallis-Osake-Pankin Kuukausikatsaus* (Helsinki), 3 (1972).
2. I am indebted for much of the material in this and the two subsequent pages to E. Pihkala, 'Suomen ulkomaankauppa vuosina 1945–72', in Perko, *Suomi toisen maailmansodan jälkeen.*
3. These figures for agriculture are given by N. Westermarck, 'Maatalouden ongelmat', ibid.
4. *Helsingin Sanomat,* 8 May 1975.
5. B–O Johansson 'SEV-yhteistyö teollisuuden kannalta' in *Suomi ja Sev,* a special issue of *Ulkopolitiikka* (Helsinki), 1974.
6. e.g. R. Tötterman's speech of 8 May 1972 in *UPLA* 1972.
7. Gronow, pp. 172–7 and 184.
8. *Katsaus* 3 (Helsinki), 1974.
9. S. Klockare, *Yleislakosta kansanrintamaan* (Helsinki, 1971), pp. 17–63; Tiainen, pp. 49ff.
10. P. Klemola, *Juuso Walden–viimeinen patruuna* (Helsinki, 1970), pp. 137–40 maintains that a large part of the wood, paper and pulp industry supported Kekkonen in 1961.
11. P. Väyrynen, *On muutoksen aika* (Porvoo–Helsinki, 1974), pp. 96–101. A detailed

account of these tax changes will be found in *Establishing a business in Finland* (Helsinki, Min. of Commerce & Industry, 1970), pp. 21–2.

12. Mentioned by Jakobson, *Finnish neutrality*, p. 27.

13. Wuorinen, pp. 382–3 and 388–92.

14. I. Harki, *Sotakorvausten aika* (Jyväskylä, 1971), p. 95 states that some 30 per cent of reparations were paid by the wood, paper and pulp industry (these products included cellulose).

15. Harki, pp. 97, 100, and 350.

16. Ibid., p. 351.

17. V. Halme, *Suomi ja maailmantalous* (Helsinki, 1962), p. 111.

18. *Turun Sanomat*, 23 Nov 1974.

19. Gronow, pp. 181–3.

20. Söderhjelm, pp. 72–93.

21. On the initial reactions of the Finnish bourgeois press, see Apunen, pp. 117–18.

22. Jakobson, *Finnish neutrality*, p. 60, speculates that 'Finland may have saved herself from Communism by saying no to the Marshall Plan'.

23. R. Väyrynen, *Conflicts in Finnish-Soviet relations* (Tampere, 1972), p. 226.

24. Ibid., pp. 90–1, 131, and 159.

25. *Turun Sanomat*, 2 Feb 1974.

26. Päiviö Hetemäki, quoted in *Helsingin Sanomat*, 5 Feb 1974.

27. TV news, 12 Feb 1974; *Uusi Suomi*, 17 Oct 1974.

28. Doubts were openly expressed in Finland about the *economic* wisdom of importing natural gas from the Soviet Union when it had raised oil prices (TV news, 14 Jan 1974).

29. *Helsingin Sanomat*, 22 Aug 1974.

30. Ibid., 26 Apr 1974.

31. *Uusi YV*, 12 (1973).

32. OECD, *Economic Survey: Finland*, 1969, p. 10.

33. Harki, p. 119.

34. Wuorinen, pp. 468–9; Harki, pp. 104–8. A. M. Salonen, *Linjat* (Helsinki, 1972), pp. 37–8, stresses that Finland benefited indirectly from Marshall Aid, especially where Swedish financial help was concerned.

35. Hyvämäki, *Kanava*, pp. 392 and 396.

36. Halme, p. 55. On Finland's foreign credits in this period see also R. Bärlund, *KOP Economic Review* (Helsinki), 4 (1961).

37. Report by T. Helilä in *Helsingin Sanomat*, 25 Jan 1969.

38. Söderhjelm, p. 109.

39. K. Törnudd, *Soviet attitudes towards non-military regional cooperation* (Helsinki, 1961), pp. 110–17.

40. The praise given to the Nordic free labour market by one of the leading Finnish politicians most committed to the protection of his country's agriculture is somewhat ironic (J. Virolainen, *Pääministerinä Suomessa*, Helsinki, 1969, pp. 201–2).

41. *Nordic Economic and Social Cooperation* (Report of Nordic Council Conference, Sept 1967, Stockholm, 1968), p. 41.

42. Speech by Aarre Simonen in *UPLA* 1956–8, p. 104.

43. Speech by Prime Minister V. J. Sukselainen, ibid., 1959, p. 50.

44. Ibid., 1959, pp. 55, 59, and 64.

45. *The Economist*, 10 Dec 1960.

46. *Talouselämä*, 1–2 (1961).

47. A. Etzioni, *Political unification* (New York, 1965), p. 221.

48. R. Rossi, 'Suomen EFTA-ongelma', *Kansantaloudellinen aikakauskirja* (Helsinki), 2 (1961).

49. e.g. N. Nilsson's statement in *Talouselämä*, 5 (1969).

50. In regard to pulp and newsprint, EFTA officials admitted that great expansion

would have occurred even without EFTA, for the existing tariffs in the EFTA countries were low (*The effects of EFTA on the economies of the member-states*, Geneva, 1969, pp. 69–71).

51. Reinikainen's statements are in *Talouselämä*, 6, 7, and 9 (1969).
52. Article by U. Luukko, ibid., 6 (1969).
53. P. Kleppe, *EFTA–Nordek–EEC* (Stockholm, 1970), pp. 48–52.
54. *Helsingin Sanomat*, 1 Feb 1975.
55. Minister T. A. Wiherheimo's statement in *UPLA* 1956–8, p. 109.
56. *Nordic cooperation in a European perspective* (Report of Nordic Council Conference, Sept 1971, Stockholm, 1972), p. 51.
57. On some of the problems of Swedish investment in Finland, see K. Bärlund and T. Lausti, *Viimeinen taisto?* (Helsinki, 1970), pp. 29–48.
58. See Reinikainen's statement in *Talouselämä*, 14 (1969).
59. Kleppe, pp. 95–8.
60. Ibid., pp. 158–71.
61. *Helsingin Sanomat*, 24 Jan 1969.
62. The Danish prime minister, H. Baunsgaard, had all along stressed that Nordek was not an alternative to EEC, but would provide better conditions for participating in European integration (Kleppe, p. 212).
63. Törnudd, p. 146.
64. *New Times*, 6, 8, and 21 (1969).
65. P. Korpinen, 'Suomen Nordek-politiikka', *Katsaus*, 1 (1975).
66. R. Väyrynen, pp. 92–6.
67. U. Luukko, *Talouselämä*, 6 (1969).
68. M. Mäenpää, *KOP Economic Review*, 3 (1972).
69. Statement by Minister O. J. Mattila in *UPLA* 1970, pp. 134–8 and by Minister P. Uusivirta, ibid., 1972, pp. 164–73.
70. By the end of autumn 1974 Finnish experts were admitting the insufficiency of the flow of foreign loan capital to Finland (TV programme *Erikoistoimitus*, 5 Dec 1974).
71. Minister J-M. Jansson in a TV interview, Jan 1974.
72. *Helsingin Sanomat*, 12 Feb 1974 and *Uusi Suomi*, 13 Mar 1974.
73. *Helsingin Sanomat*, 29 Jan 1974.
74. Fears of EEC pulp and paper users of being at the mercy of the Finnish industry were expressed in *The Economist*, 4 May 1974, and, as far as the Germans were concerned, by a leading German business representative on Finnish TV on 4 Dec 1974.
75. *Helsingin Sanomat*, 11 Sept 1973. Hetemäki also argued, however, that the Finnish wood, paper and pulp industry could not long stand Swedish, Norwegian and Austrian competition if it remained outside a free-trade agreement with EEC permanently (*Turun Sanomat*, 13 Apr 1973).
76. *Tuotantouutiset*, 2–3 (1974).
77. Voitto Ahonen, TV news, 2 May 1974.
78. Jermu Laine, quoted in *Helsingin Sanomat*, 8 June 1973.
79. Ibid., 13 June 1975.
80. T. Hiltunen, *KOP Economic Review*, 2 (1975).

FROM what has been said in the preceding chapter, it should be clear that in Finland's external policy economic questions have come increasingly to the fore in the post-World War II world, and especially in the last decade and a half. Because the Finns have strong commercial relations with both the East and West, Finnish neutrality has, somewhat paradoxically, become the expression of the concrete reality that Finland's economy is tied to both sides. As previously noted, the Finns have suffered disadvantages as well as having gained advantages from their economic relations with both the Western and Socialist countries. In an integrating Europe they feel that they must seek a fruitful relationship with every economic bloc while avoiding domination by any. This outlook gives content to the external policy of neutrality, and also reflects the compromises of the internal political scene. Illustrative of the situation is Finland's agreement with the EEC, bitterly opposed as it was by a section of the Left. The fact that this agreement had to be limited to trade and that no 'development' paragraph was written into it, has meant, among other things, that the Finns have avoided any automatic influx of foreign labour into their country that might have occurred if a more extensive relationship with the EEC had been agreed upon. It is noteworthy that until recently there was a growing labour shortage in Finland—and this at a time when unemployment elsewhere in Europe was rising. Thus in practical terms neutrality for Finland means something more than being simply bound economically to both sides. It means that the bonds are not of the tightest, that there is lee-way or manœuverability. Neutrality affords some protection for Finland—which is, in many respects, an isolated country, many of whose inhabitants are not ripe for wider schemes of integration—from the too rapid pressures of European change.

In a European crisis, particularly one of an extreme political-military nature, Finland's diverse economic links, not to speak of other factors, make it extremely vulnerable. As far as Finland's imports of energy are concerned, the Soviet Union's power to exercise control in such a crisis, either as a result of Finnish dependence on Soviet supplies or of a Soviet ability to stop supplies coming into Finland from elsewhere, would seem to be very great. In this situation the utmost that could be expected of neutrality is a neutrality benevolent to the Soviet Union. It is significant that in such a crisis period Swedish neutrality, too, would be under comparable pressures, though from the Western side. Talking on his country's TV on 13 March 1975, the Swedish foreign minister expressed the opinion that Sweden's neutrality was already being rendered more difficult by economic dependence on the West, especially in regard to the need to secure oil flows through the International Energy Agency. In a crisis affecting Northern Europe these weaknesses in Finnish and Swedish neutrality increase considerably the speed at which polarization in Northern Europe would occur.

The fundamental concern of Finnish foreign policy must therefore continue to be the search for political security. Historically Finland's security problem has been the conflict, latent or actual, with Russia, where the way of life, both in the pre- and post-1917 world, has always been vastly different from that to which the Finns have been accustomed. Though, also historically, the Finns did reach a *modus vivendi* with the Russians for a large part of the nineteenth century, this fact, when taken into account with the tremendous efforts made by the Finns since World War II to come to terms with the needs of the Soviet Union, only serves to emphasize the underlying problem, presented by Russia's proximity to Finland's existence as a state.

In coming to terms with the Soviet Union, the Paasikivi-Kekkonen foreign policy has shown so great an understanding of Russia's security concern to protect its north-western frontier that the Finns are committed to defend this frontier against an attack through Finland by Germany or its allies. In addition Kekkonen's foreign policy has broadened after 1961 to embrace the promotion of wider measures that serve essential Finnish interests and, often also, those of the Soviet Union (though it should be remembered that there are Finnish démarches such as, for example, the 1971 German 'package deal' that apparently came as unheralded to the Russians as to the Western powers). The traditional Finnish-Russian conflict occurred, as noted in earlier chapters, within the framework of a larger Western-Russian and in particular German-Russian conflict, and it is clear that the Finns, in agreeing to settle their own conflict with Russia, primarily through the 1948 Treaty, have moved over to the Russian side in many important respects as far as this larger conflict of Russia with the West is concerned.

Having said this, however, it at once becomes necessary to point out the qualifications in Finland's position vis-à-vis the Soviet Union: that the military clauses of the treaty are limited to an attack upon or through Finland, that Finland is not a member of the Warsaw Pact, and that in a crisis in Europe the Finns will endeavour to maintain their neutrality. These are the limits set by the Finns in their military-political relationship with the Soviet Union in a crisis situation. However fragile such limits may turn out to be in the reality of a crisis situation, their existence serves to indicate that the Finns not merely fear embroilment in a general European war, but that for them the security of their country would not depend upon a Soviet victory (as it would in the case of the governments of Eastern Europe), for if the security of Finland did depend on a Soviet victory in a European war, then the Finnish aim would be the maximum possible and not the minimum possible military relationship with the Soviet Union. The fact that many Finnish spokesmen have continually stressed the ability of their country's armed forces to fulfil the obligations of the 1948 Treaty unaided does indicate that in a crisis situation Finland's traditional security problem with Russia would by no means have disappeared. The friendship of the Soviet Union which the treaty, its exploitation by the Finns, as well as Kekkonen's own démarches, have ultimately secured, has replaced the old Finnish-Russian antagonism, but security problems for the Finns reside in the ease with which the Soviet Union could now act in regard to Finland.

Since the 1948 security treaty, valuable though it might be, cannot give complete security, but, on the contrary, may create serious dilemmas of how far in a crisis situation to go unaided, to go with Russia, or to go against the West, the Finnish leaders are driven to look for solutions to Finland's security problem in the improvement of relations between the states and, in particular, between the major powers. In this improvement the Finns themselves claim to have played a modest role. Above all this has meant working within the context of the détente in Europe, and hence a correspondence between many of the Finnish démarches and Soviet interests has been inevitable.

The Finns have nevertheless pursued several specific objectives of their own. In the 1948 Treaty Germany was named as the possible enemy. A few months after the treaty was signed the initial troubles of the 1948-50 Fagerholm government occurred at the time of the first Berlin blockade. The 1958 'night-frost crisis' ran on into the period of the second Berlin blockade, while the 'note crisis' of 1961 came at the latter end of the third Berlin crisis.[1] It thus became an understandable endeavour of the Finns, once they themselves came to admit how inextricably bound up with German affairs their fortunes were, to seek an alleviation of their position from the German side. But it was not until 1971, by which time Brandt's Ostpolitik was already proving itself, that the Finns were able to tackle this problem directly by means of their so-called 'German package-deal'. This rather sudden reversal of the Finnish policy pursued hitherto—which had been to refuse, in the name of neutrality, to have diplomatic relations with either of the two Germanies—was intended in large part to strengthen Finnish neutrality at one of its most vulnerable points. For if the potential enemy Germany (1948 Treaty—nowadays in practice West Germany), could be got to recognize Finnish neutrality, then the *raison d'être* for the 1948 Treaty would hardly be as compelling. The reception of the 'German package' was not quite as smooth as the Finns had hoped. Nevertheless the understanding shown towards Finnish neutrality by both the Germanies, and the appearance of the delegates of both German states at Helsinki in the first and third sessions of the European Security Conference (where the delegations sat side by side) have provided the Finns with ample evidence of an improvement in the German situation that is bound to have a beneficial effect on Finland's position.

As a further precaution against the calamity of a European or indeed global conflict, the Finns have been seriously trying for over a decade to get guarantees for the 'contracting out' of Northern Europe from the potential conflict area—endeavours which obviously connect closely with the desire to get recognition of Finnish neutrality from the Federal Republic of Germany. The most striking Finnish proposal has been for the creation of a North European nuclear-free zone. This proposal has brought the Finns a certain amount of infamy in NATO quarters, for it so evidently echoes the earlier ideas of Soviet and East European leaders, and would seem to have the effect of sapping still further Norway's commitment to NATO. But the Finns, who have hosted some of the SALT talks, are well aware of the possibility of working within the broad framework of US-Soviet relations in this question. In actual fact the agreement for the prevention of nuclear war concluded between the United States and the Soviet Union in 1973 has been interpreted by one Soviet authority as indicating the willingness of the parties to strive for the creation of nuclear-free zones.[2] In recent months the Finns seemed to have turned more and more to the idea of having the superpowers guarantee a nuclear-free Northern Europe. In spite of a certain air of Utopianism in thinking of this kind, such ideas do relate essentially to a Finnish hope that in a crisis situation the Finnish armed forces will be able to hold their country intact, untroubled by major aggression, whatever happens elsewhere in Europe.

Finnish concern for the promotion of the European Security Conference and its follow-up has reference to the problem of how to deal with any future crises in Finland's foreign relations, and the hosting of the initial and final sessions of the Security Conference as well as the work done behind the scenes and in committees by the Finns should not be ascribed simply to a desire to win prestige for their country. The opportunity to refer to a set of principles in a threatening conflict situation has much significance for the Finns. It has been a source of strength in the postwar world that they have felt able to negotiate with the Russians in crisis periods and have not simply capitulated to the initial Soviet demands. By negotiating calmly in 1948 about the nature of their security treaty with the Soviet Union, modifications in the Soviet-Finnish treaty were gained by the Finns so that their treaty differs considerably from the Soviet-Romanian treaty. The Romanians, for example, have a very wide commitment to take action with the Soviet Union 'to obviate any threat of renewed aggression by Germany or any other power which might be associated with Germany either directly or in any other way.' Again in 1961, by talking to the Russians about the danger of the spread of 'war psychosis' throughout the rest of the Scandinavian peninsula should the Soviet leaders persist in their demand for military consultations, the Finnish statesmen were able to appeal to an element in Soviet thinking—and even to the very phraseology used by the Soviet authorities—that was immensely advantageous to the Finnish case. These facts should be borne in mind when assessing Finland's deep involvement in the European Security Conference and its final declaration of principles.

Above all the European Security Conference, which functioned on the principles of consensus and the equality of states, had the virtue in Finnish eyes of fostering the development of multilateral contacts on a meaningful level. Considering the excessively bilateral nature of Finland's foreign relations during much of the postwar period, this Finnish preoccupation is understandable. One of Finland's leading experts on international relations, Professor Göran von Bonsdorff, himself a former chairman of the Finnish-Soviet Friendship Society, has for some time urged the growing importance of multilateral contacts and stressed that the relationship of dependence in these contacts does not depend on the power position of one state towards another. On the other hand, says Bonsdorff, in a bilateral relationship between states of uneven strength there is a danger of the larger state pressurizing the smaller so as to render its freedom to negotiate more or less illusory.[3]

All Finnish leaders are, however, aware that their scope for action depends on the existence of détente in Europe. Since the progress of détente has depended very much upon initiatives from the Soviet side, it is easy on this account alone to assume that Finnish policy is inhibited by consciousness of a need not to disturb the Soviet Union's détente policy. This may be true, but it is difficult to see what the Finns could in practice gain from, say, complaining about the Murmansk base. On the other hand, many North European leaders feel that certain Finnish spokesmen go too far in their expression of pro-Soviet feelings. The call for Soviet participation in North European economic cooperation made by the left-wing Social Democrat M.P., Erkki Tuomioja, at the Reykjavik meeting of the Nordic Council in February 1975 upset not merely Swedish and Norwegian delegates but also members of the Finnish delegation. Nevertheless Tuomioja was not putting forward a mere personal opinion: his viewpoint had some support among a section, albeit a minority, of his party.

It is at this point that the charge of Finlandization might seem to have most relevance. The question is whether the increasingly positive Finnish-Soviet relationship has led to the slow penetration of Finland by Soviet values. The history of post-1948 Finland certainly proves that for the Soviet government the existence of a security treaty with Finland is not enough in itself. The Russians must be convinced that they will have in Finland a government loyal to the obligations and spirit of the treaty. The three crises of 1948–1950, 1958, and 1961 all show in varying degrees the problem the Soviet government has in trusting the Finnish political system, for the essence of the present Finnish-Soviet relationship is that it is nevertheless based upon a Soviet feeling that support can be found within the untransformed Finnish system. Since this has led the Soviet government, on occasion, to show its preferences within that system—in the last decade and a half for Kekkonen ahead of anyone else—it might seem natural to assume that the system will gradually change in consequence of this influence, even though the original Soviet intention was to accept the system as such (until, of course, the day of the long-deferred Communist millennium).

Some evidence does indeed exist of the adaptability of the Finnish system towards a closer rapprochement with the Soviet outlook. It was noteworthy that after Allende's fall Kekkonen delivered an address to the Faculty of Law of the University of Turku on 14 September 1973, in which he quoted Lenin on the absurdity of expecting a smooth transition to social reform by parliamentary means under circumstances like those prevailing in Chile. This was a somewhat astonishing line to take, since part of the feeling of outrage that swept Finland at the time of Allende's overthrow was inspired by the sympathy Finns had for an attempt to create fundamental social and economic change by peaceful, constitutional means. Nor could Kekkonen have ever been visualized quoting Lenin in, say, his earlier terms of office. Commentators on both the radio and TV networks have in recent years been open in their criticism of the sins of US imperialism, while ignoring the labour camps of the USSR, preferring instead to dwell on the merits of the latter's school system.

The most important phenomenon remains that of self-censorship, which has had some effect upon the whole of the Finnish community. In seeking to explain why this should have arisen, Max Jakobson, bearing in mind a powerful attack in a British journal by one of his fellow countrymen against self-censorship,[4] has pointed out that in Finland foreign policy has demanded and achieved the support of the whole nation, who are aware of the main objectives of that policy and the difficulties it has had to contend with in its formation.[5] Rather than give vent to expressions of hostility about other countries' political systems, many Finns prefer to identify with their own country's constructive work in the field of international affairs. President Kekkonen himself has claimed to act as a bridge-builder in international relations.[6] This image has also had its effect on the outlook of several Finnish institutions. The SAK, for example, has done its own share of bridge-building in recent years[7] in attempting to effect a rapprochement between the trade union movements of Western Europe and the Socialist countries, especially the Soviet Union. In this the special relationship that Finland has with the Soviet Union as well as Finland's own neutrality have been positive factors. But in the last resort the trade union leaders feel that the success of this work rests upon the support given by the rank and file of the movement. It was therefore characteristic of the Finnish outlook that in a talk delivered at Tampere on 4 May 1973 the International Secretary of SAK, Kari Tapiola, took as his theme 'the way in which citizens' associations can strengthen the main lines of Finnish foreign policy', for what is involved in this kind of activity is a patriotic endeavour in which every citizen can play a role.

Though Paasikivi would have been at best indifferent to work of this kind, the concern of Finns nowadays to promote cooperation between the West and the Soviet Union, and to pay the price by abstaining from criticism of the Soviet Union, stems essentially from the ultimate success of Paasikivi's own policy of convincing the Finns that Soviet objectives as far as Finland was concerned were limited to the need to ensure the security of the Soviet Union's north-eastern frontier. Stable societies of the Western parliamentary type—such a society Finland is nowadays—have aimed at a high degree of internal consensus as far as their external policy is concerned. But in postwar Finland this consensus was difficult to achieve, particularly as Finnish foreign policy-makers demanded recognition of the need for friendship with the Soviet Union, the power that had defeated Finland and, in the Cold War years, was the recipient of the opprobrium of every other Western land. Since postwar reconstruction in Finland involved also the emergence into legality of a powerful Communist Party, it seemed to many Finns that the stability of the country was threatened equally from within. This view affected not merely bourgeois Finns, but the Social Democrats too, who retained under Tanner a strong pro-Western orientation. As rivalry between the Agrarians and the Social Democrats increased in the 50s over the apportioning of the national product between rural and urban interests, a new dimension was added to the problem of achieving wide support for the country's foreign policy, since by this time the Agrarians had become the element in the Finnish political system on which the Russians placed their trust. Not until the mid-60s, when the attitude of the Social Democratic Party began to change towards the Agrarians (Centre Party), Communists, and the Soviet Union, was the scene set for the achievement of near-consensus in foreign policy. What the Social Democrats had come to recognize was that Finland's parliamentary system had been retained but with a different alignment of forces within it. This recognition also paved the way for a certain radicalization of Finnish society, and this radicalization in turn made its own demands on Finnish foreign policy.

The détente in Europe encouraged many Finns, particularly those of the younger generation active in party politics and journalism, to see the problems of the world in terms others than those of a conflict between Communism and Western parliamentary democracy—the stabilizing of Finnish-Soviet relations seeming to show that the latter conflict was anyway reducible to manageable proportions. By the end of the 60s the Finnish Foreign Office was being pressed by radical elements to recognize North Vietnam, but Finnish official policy did not at this time go to the lengths of Swedish policy in this question, though in 1975 the Finns were quicker off the mark than the Swedes to establish diplomatic relations with the People's Republic of South Vietnam. The fact nevertheless was that while the Finns avoided the kind of quarrel the Swedes had with the United States—a quarrel that led to the withdrawal of the American ambassador to Sweden—Kekkonen still went so far as to single out, in a speech to the students of the University of Turku on 9 November 1972, the Americans' waging of war in Vietnam as an example of a cruel and totally negative war that neutral states should condemn. This direct criticism of an important aspect of a superpower's foreign policy was something new. The Finnish attitude to the Soviet invasions of Hungary (1956) and Czechoslovakia (1968) and, hitherto, to the American presence on the South-East Asia mainland had been to demand in all cases the withdrawal of foreign troops while avoiding allegations of blame towards the superpower concerned.

A further case of anti-Americanism in the Finnish outlook came with the fall of Allende. In the spring of 1974 the Finns hosted an international commission that investigated the atrocities committed by the Chilean junta. The commission was addressed by the prime minister, Kalevi Sorsa (though not in his capacity as prime minister): he said that it was the duty of the international community, on the basis of the principles on which the United Nations was founded, to see to it that fundamental rights were restored in Chile.[8] In a twenty-minute audience with several of the leading members of the commission President Kekkonen went even further and promised that Finland would give all possible support to the restoration of democracy in Chile.[9] Nevertheless these Finnish statements, including those also of the radical minister of education, Ulf Sundqvist (who played a large part in organizing the commission's sittings in Finland) fell short this time of an open condemnation of US policy.

In assessing this radical input in Finnish foreign policy pronouncements, care should be taken to see it as essentially reflecting a concern for small nations and states, and the case both of Vietnam and Chile should be seen as symbols for the Finns of nations struggling to achieve internal reforms but disturbed in this by foreign interference. It should be remembered that all political parties, including the Communists, condemned on its occurrence the invasion of Czechoslovakia by Warsaw Pact troops in 1968. But viewpoints of this kind, whether directed against the Russians or the Americans, should not be regarded as upsetting the basic conviction on which Finnish foreign policy operates, namely that constructive policy cannot be pursued without recognition of the reality and even legitimacy of the primary interests of the great powers, and especially of the superpowers.

Finland in the United Nations

It is in Finland's UN policy that the attempt to reconcile, on the one hand, an interest in the fate of small states and nations, and on the other an appreciation of the needs of the great powers, can best be seen. In his blueprint for the post-1944 world Pekka Peitsi criticized the League of Nations for the anarchy it brought as a result of reliance on the doctrine of the equality of states. He envisaged the creation of a postwar world organization that would certainly recall the League in many respects, but in which the great powers would not have their action fettered by the unbridled sovereignty of the smaller states.[10] Yet smaller states, whose rights were recognized by the Atlantic Charter—the propaganda value of which Peitsi hoped the Soviet government would take note of[11]— had to find their place too.

For many years it looked as if Finland would never find its own place. From 1947 to the end of 1955 the question of Finland's admission to the UN remained unresolved, for while, during this period, the West refused to accept the admission of Bulgaria, Romania, Hungary, and Mongolia, the Soviet Union retaliated by opposing on principle the admission of other states, including

Finland.[12] At the same time it has to be conceded that President Paasikivi was not an enthusiast for the UN,[13] his scepticism undoubtedly influenced by the failure of the League. When Finland arrived in the UN in 1956, as a result of the 'package deal' of autumn 1955, Finnish policy was devised to proceed with great caution, bearing in mind the need to impress upon the world that Finland was a neutral state. A large part of home opinion was thus dissatisfied with what was considered to be the too timid attitude of the Finnish delegate in the UN debate on the Soviet invasion of Hungary.[14] It was some years before the Finns were able to shape a UN policy that won the understanding of the majority of the nation by showing that Finnish attitudes expressed in the UN were a true reflection of the role the organization could play to promote 'international peace and security'—these were the terms the Finnish government had originally used to the Finnish parliament in justifying Finland's application for admission to the UN in early 1947.[15] And twenty years later Karjalainen re-stated these terms as 'the primary task' of the UN.[16]

Finnish UN policy has been characterized by a strong respect for the Security Council, on which Max Jakobson sat in 1969–70 (while the principle of universality—the principle that has made the European Security Conference so important for the Finns—was enshrined in the UN in the General Assembly, and on the grounds of this principle the Finns have not supported the exclusion of South Africa from the Assembly). For the Finns the Security Council embodies—when it is working at its best—the concept of a great power unanimity shared with the representatives of smaller states. The Finnish viewpoint has tended to be resistant to the enthusiasms of the General Assembly, where such enthusiasms might upset any great power interests. All Finnish leaders, and especially Jakobson, have been only too well aware of Molotov's remark about the interests of his country being thwarted in the League of Nations by the behaviour of a country like Bolivia.[17]

And so while Finnish foreign policy-makers had to convince the Finnish nation of the value of being in the UN, they had at the same time to devise a role that would show demonstrable results without alienating the feelings of the powers. The fact was that it was impossible for the Finns to remain passive in the UN, however much the older conservative-minded diplomats may have desired passivity. On 10 December 1957 Finland received a note from the Soviet Union asking for the support of Finland *as a UN member* in the cause of working against the growing threat of war in the world. The Finns had thus to declare themselves, and two days later Ralph Enckell addressed the UN Assembly with a statement of the Finnish attitude to world problems. In a reference to the Cold War, Enckell stated that his fellow countrymen would be happier if the terms 'east' and 'west' could be simply regarded as geographical expressions. Quoting a statement made previously in connection with the visit of Bulganin and Khrushchev to Finland, Enckell went on to explain his country's policy as being motivated by a need to avoid anything that might promote disagreement in the world, and correspondingly his country worked for everything that brought the nations together and would remove the points of conflict between them. A more striking version of the same theme was contained in Kekkonen's address to the UN on 19 October 1961. On that occasion Kekkonen tried to project the image of Finland as a doctor, diagnosing and trying to cure. This rather pompous imagery hid a Finnish fear of being caught up as a participant in an international controversy: better a physician than a judge was Kekkonen's basic standpoint.

The first clear issuance from this policy did not come till the appointment of Sakari Tuomioja as UN mediator in Cyprus in 1964, but highly characteristic of Finland's approach to the UN has been its willingness to supply peacekeeping forces for areas of tension, a policy beginning in Suez in 1956, when the Finnish Major-General A. E. Martola served as military adviser to Dag Hammarskjöld, and continuing to the present day, when a Finn, General E. Siilasvuo, has been UN commander in Suez, the Finns having in addition played a prominent role in the peacekeeping forces throughout the period of troubles in Cyprus, where Martola also served as UN commander. In these cases the Finnish role, under UN auspices, has been to perform tasks that the great powers themselves would have difficulty in performing. Where such work was liable to run too close to great power conflicts, however, the Finns have not wished for involvement—they did not supply peacekeeping forces for the Congo dispute.

Nevertheless by the 1960s the Finns had come to the realization that neutral states and their representatives might act creditably in many areas of international activity without running the risk of antagonizing a single great power. In his 1957 statement to the UN Enckell had defined his country as being, like the other Northern European countries, a society based upon respect for human dignity and the rights of the individual, a country in which the rule of law was paramount. It is hardly surprising therefore to find that a number of Finns have been prominent in UN work that has involved the careful defining of rights and the limitation of power. In 1975, after several years of work, a UN committee under the chairmanship of Professor Bengt Broms of the University of Helsinki finally arrived at a definition of aggression, and Broms was soon after appointed to chair another committee set to re-examine and where necessary re-draft the UN Charter. Other Finns have served the UN in the field of disarmament (Ilkka Pastinen), in women's rights (Helvi Sipilä), and in the examination of the problems posed by multinational companies (Klaus Sahlgren), and so on. This detailed work of a legal and technical nature, however specialized it may seem to be, does exemplify a utilization of the same kind of qualities that were called forth in the Finnish promotion of and preparations for the European Security Conference. There is, throughout this aspect of Finnish endeavour, a fundamental conviction in the ability to produce results by patient discussion and compromise, work that aims, in short, at the resolution of conflict by multilateral activity.

However, when in 1967 Helvi Sipilä, in welcoming the International Year of Human Rights, defined her country as one 'in which human rights and freedoms have been deeply appreciated for centuries'[18] it was already evident that a certain tension existed between the professed Finnish concern for rights and several other of the leading postulates on which Finnish UN policy was built. A few months earlier Jakobson had stated that his country's neutrality enabled the Finns 'to maintain good relations with all states across the dividing lines of ideology or military alignments'.[19] But which principle was to determine Finnish reactions to the increasing demands voiced in the General Assembly by the Afro-Asian states for resolutions and action about apartheid—a non-ideological neutrality or a concern for the establishment of human rights? A few months after his UN pronouncement on Finnish neutrality, Jakobson expressed himself, in the UN special political committee on apartheid policy, as being weary of the continual resolutions put through the General Assembly about apartheid, for the Security Council was not acting upon them.[20] In fact Jakobson's attitude was dictated more by a consciousness of the futility of such activity than by a distaste for the content of the resolutions. Finnish policy on apartheid had already undergone a change since the years when Finnish attitudes on this question were more restrained than those expressed by other North European nations.[21] This change was the product of several pressures—of the growing cooperation in the UN between Finland and the other North European states and of the radicalization of thinking in Finland about international questions. But above all the change was necessitated as a natural consequence of the growing involvement of Finland in UN work.

By the middle 60s Finnish appreciation of the value of the UN as a forum and contact-point between the states had risen considerably. Before the signing of the NPT of 1968, Jakobson's services were much employed by the United States and the Soviet Union to secure understanding of the aims of the treaty in the UN,[22] while his work for the passing of Security Council Resolution 255 has already been noted in chapter 3. Some time before this activity, when it had been rumoured in the middle of the decade that U Thant might not accept a further term of office, the names of both Enckell and Jakobson had been unofficially mentioned as possible successors.[23] If the Finns were to be in a position to utilize the UN, however, it was essential to have good relations not merely with the great powers but also with the Afro-Asian majority in the General Assembly. By the late 60s Finnish UN policy had begun to show an especial concern for the deterioration of conditions in Namibia (a part of Africa where the Finns had been engaged in missionary enterprise since the nineteenth century). Jakobson himself got the Namibia question referred for the second time to the Hague International Court, which on this occasion gave a ruling against South Africa, thus soothing the African states and winning prestige for Finland and Jakobson without disturbing the Western powers and their interests. Indeed Jakobson, who was from 1966 a member and chairman of the UN Special Committee, which dealt, *inter alia*, with peacekeeping problems, had become something of an adept at finding ways out of impasses between great power and small power interests. As Finland's representative on the Security Council, he found the right formula to get Ireland's views on the Ulster question heard by the Council.[24] In short, in the person of Max Jakobson, Finnish foreign policy had developed a sense of its own value, and it is hardly surprising that his own strivings and those of his country culminated in 1971 in his candidacy for the post of UN Secretary-General.

There is no doubt that the election of Jakobson would have been regarded by the Finnish Foreign Office as an important strengthening element in Finnish security policy. His candidacy was launched at a time when there was much concern in Finnish foreign policy to widen Finland's international standing and to secure as manifold a recognition as possible of Finnish neutrality. Jakobson's chances appeared to be good. Finnish-Soviet relations were excellent, while on the other hand Jakobson was well respected in political circles in the eastern United States and by American and British diplomats. He had championed the People's Republic of China's right to a seat on the Security Council and his standing among the nations of the Third World was high—in spite of his Jewish origin, even some of the Arab states were not opposed to his candidature.[25]

The Leftist critics of Finnish foreign policy saw in Jakobson's candidature an attempt to strengthen Finland's position in the world by exalting Finnish neutrality so as to diminish the bilateralism engendered by the treaty relationship with the USSR.[26] Many factors point to the fundamental truth of this viewpoint, however crudely it may at times have been expressed. Both Jakobson and his promoter Hyvärinen had ambitious ideas about Finnish neutrality and both had many Western contacts—and very few contacts with the Soviet Union, whose acceptance of the candidature was erroneously assumed, as if the Soviet Union could be presented with a situation it would find difficult to counter.

On the other hand the Leftist viewpoint that President Kekkonen had in some way become duped by a technocratic inner circle of Foreign Office officials can hardly be accepted.[27] Not merely has Kekkonen ultimate responsibility under the Finnish constitution for foreign policy, but we have noted that he has certainly exercised that responsibility. It is hardly coincidental either that the German 'package-deal'—aiming, among other things, at the promotion of Finnish neutrality among the powers as well as Germany—was concocted at the time of Jakobson's candidature.

When Jakobson fell as a result of the Soviet veto, Kekkonen remained, his flexible outlook and long identification with the policy of good relations between Finland and the Soviet Union ensuring that no break in these relations would occur. Indeed there was no evidence from the Soviet side that the Soviet government was dissatisfied with the nature of Finnish-Soviet relations as such, from which it may be assumed that the obstacle resided either in Jakobson personally or in some aspect of his country's policy outside the Finnish-Soviet relationship. As far as Jakobson's ethnic background was in question, it is certain that two of the Soviet Union's closest supporters in the Middle East, Syria and Iraq, were strongly opposed to the candidature, with lesser degrees of opposition being manifested by several other Arab states, but on the other hand the Afro-Asian nations were largely sympathetic to Jakobson, at least initially. It is highly likely that the Soviet Union's veto was enforced less out of a concern for the USSR's relations with particular states than from fear of once more having a powerful UN Secretary-General—a second Dag Hammarskjöld—who was in general Western-orientated and who had the backing of a small state with an ambitious foreign policy.

In the failure of Jakobson's candidature a small state's capacity to manipulate an international political structure reached its limits (Jakobson's candidature had been ardently canvassed by the Finns among the Western powers, while the Austrians had not pushed Waldheim's candidature in the same way and on the whole had pursued a much more restrained foreign policy). The limits to Finnish action were once again set by great power politics, in brief, by the same great power that had constrained Finnish action in the past. But Finland, as the success of the European Security Conference showed, had lost the trust neither of the latter great power nor of any other. The success of this conference also showed that the Finns had not lost their ability to promote their own interests within a multilateral framework.

Since 1941 Finnish foreign policy in its broad lines has shown a growing understanding of the dominance of the great powers in the world. The commitment to work with Germany in 1941 was gradually and painfully transformed at the end of the war and in the postwar world into a commitment to help to reduce the polarization that hitherto existed between Germany and Russia. No less than the Soviet leaders the Finns at heart prefer the bipolarization in the world between the United States and the Soviet Union to an intense bipolarization in Europe between the Soviet Union and Germany. If, for example, a strong Murmansk base can be accepted as a part of a world nuclear polarization between the Soviet Union and the United States, it is a better outlook for the Finns than the view that sees the base developing as a challenge to Western Europe, to West German rearmament, etc., a view that directly focuses attention upon Northern Europe and makes Finland's North European nuclear-free zone proposal seem like a proposition for unilateral disarmament.

In any case, within a world dominated by both super-power

rivalry and negotiation, the Finns feel obliged to strive constantly to improve their own security by supporting the creation of a multilateral framework for détente. If nothing else, Jakobson's candidature was a testimony to the genuineness and native character of this striving.

Notes

1. Thögersen, p. 118, believes that the steam was taken out of the Berlin crisis before the note to Finland was delivered.
2. V. Levin, *Ulkopolitiikka*, 1 (1975), p. 46. There is no specific mention of nuclear-free zones in this agreement, however.
3. G. v. Bonsdorff, *Euroopan tulevaisuus* (Helsinki, 1972), pp. 38–9.
4. C-G Lilius, 'Self-censorship in Finland', *Index on Censorship*, spring 1975.
5. M. Jakobson, 'Itsesensuurista', *Kanava*, 3 (1975).
6. A Swedish edition of Kekkonen's speeches has been published under the title of *Brobygge* (Bridge-building) (Tammerfors, 1969).
7. *Helsingin Sanomat*, 6 Oct 1973. I am grateful to Kari Tapiola for additional information.
8. *Kansan Uutiset*, 22 Mar 1974.
9. *Hufvudstadsbladet*, 23 Mar 1974.
10. Pekka Peitsi, pp. 63–4.
11. Ibid., p. 52.
12. K. Törnudd, *Suomi ja Yhdistyneet Kansakunnat* (Helsinki, 1967), pp. 27–8. Törnudd seems inclined to blame the West for generally delaying admissions.
13. K. Killinen, *Pääsihteerikilpa* (Helsinki, 1973), pp. 122–3.
14. Anckar, pp. 82–5.
15. Törnudd, p. 27.
16. *The Finnish White Book on UN Activity for 1967*, pp. 148–52.
17. Jakobson, *Diplomacy of the Winter War*, p. 82.
18. *Finnish White Book . . .*, pp. 251–3.
19. Ibid., pp. 18–19.
20. Ibid., pp. 177–9.
21. Törnudd, pp. 94–7.
22. Killinen, p. 148.
23. S. Määttänen, *Tapaus Jakobson* (Helsinki, 1973), pp. 160–4; Killinen, p. 147.
24. A. Boyd, *Fifteen men on a powder keg* (London, 1971), p. 327.
25. Killinen, p. 165. Algeria and Morocco were in favour of Jakobson.
26. Some of these criticisms are quoted, albeit disapprovingly, by Killinen, pp. 192–4.
27. Määttänen, pp. 95–6.

NOTE ON SOURCES

In the preparation of this study it has not been possible to use archive material, though to some extent material garnered from interviews, correspondence, memoranda, and official publications, has served to supplement this deficiency.

Reports in the following Finnish newspapers have been of great value for the writing of this work: the *Helsingin Sanomat*, *Uusi Suomi*, *Hufvudstadsbladet*, *Kansan Uutiset*, *Aamulehti*, and *Turun Sanomat*. In addition the Finnish journals *Ulkopolitiikka*, *Ydin*, *Talouselämä*, the *KOP Economic Review* and *Kuukausikatsaus*, and the North European journal *Cooperation and Conflict* have been frequently consulted.

The Economist has proved to be the most valuable guide for British views on Finnish affairs.

For Soviet viewpoints, the *New Times* has been surveyed since it originally appeared as *The War and the Working Class*. The Moscow journal *International Affairs* has also been of value.

Kekkonen's speeches, as well as the statements of other Finnish leaders, can be found (unless otherwise referred to) in the *Helsingin Sanomat* edition of the following day. His main speeches are published in the four volumes of *Puheita ja kirjoituksia*, ed. by T. Vilkuna and published by Weilin & Göös. Some of these have been translated into English and published in *Neutrality*, 1st ed. 1970, enlarged ed. 1973, published by Heinemann. Paasikivi's speeches for the period 1944–56 are to be found in *Paasikiven linja*, vol. i, published by Werner Soderström. Khrushchev's speeches about Northern Europe may be found in N. S. Hruštšev, *Neuvostoliitto ja Pohjola*, published by Weilin & Göös.

Of great value have been the following series published by the Finnish Foreign Office: *Ulkopoliittisia lausuntoja ja asiakirjoja* (referred to in the text as *UPLA* for the appropriate year—speeches otherwise referred to by date in the text can generally be found in these volumes, which contain both speeches and documents), the Finnish *White Books on UN Activity*, and the many volumes of *Suomi ulkomaiden lehdistössä* (for foreign press reports on Finnish matters). For North European affairs *Nordisk udredningsserie* reports have been most useful. The OECD material on Finland contained in the yearly *Economic Surveys* has also proved valuable.

Note: I should like to single out for special mention M. Häikiö's unpublished paper, *Suomen molemmille Saksan hallituksille tekemän neuvottelutarjouksen sisältö ja tausta*, written in 1971, which has greatly helped to clarify my own outlook on Finnish foreign policy.

BIBLIOGRAPHY

Ahtokari, R. *Asekätkentäjuttu.* Porvoo-Helsinki, 1971.

Anckar, D. *Partiopinioner och utrikespolitik.* Åbo, Acta Academiae Aboensis, Ser. A, no. 41, 1971.

Apunen, O. *Kansallinen realismi ja puolueettomuus Suomen ulkopoliittisina valintoina.* Tampere, Univ. of Tampere Inst. of Pol. Sci. Research Reports, no. 28, 1972, vol. i.

Assarsson, V. *Stalinin varjossa.* Porvoo-Helsinki, 1963.

Bärlund, K. & Lausti, T. *Viimeinen taisto?* Helsinki, 1970.

Blomberg, J. & Joenniemi, P. *Kaksiteräinen miekka.* Helsinki, 1971.

Bonsdorff, G. v. *Euroopan tulevaisuus.* Helsinki, 1972.

Boyd, A. *Fifteen men on a powder keg.* London, 1971.

Brodin, K. *Finlands utrikespolitiska doktrin.* Stockholm, 1971.

— 'Quo vadis, Finlandia?', *Internationella studier* (Stockholm), no. 4, 1973.

Broms, B., 'Finland and the League of Nations' in *Essays on Finnish foreign policy.* Vammala, 1963.

— *Itävallan pysyvän puolueettomuuden kehitys ja jäsenyys Yhdistyneissä Kansakunnissa* (Turku), 2 (1968).

— *Suomen puolueettomuus ja Pariisin Rauhansopimuksen sekä YYA:n sotilaspoliittiset määräykset* (offprint from Parivartio).

Bruntland, A. O. 'The Nordic balance', *Cooperation and Conflict* (Oslo), 2 (1966).

Churchill, W. *The history of the Second World War.* London, 1948-54. Vol. v.

EFTA Secretariat. *The effects of EFTA on the economies of the member-states.* Geneva, 1969.

Etzioni, A. *Political unification.* New York, 1965.

Galtung, J. *The European Community.* London, 1973.

Gräsbeck, K. 'Les fondements de la neutralité finlandaise', *Revue des Deux Mondes*, 1 Dec. 1969.

Gripenberg, G. A. *Neutralitetstanken i Finlands politik.* Stockholm, 1960.

Gronow, J. *Monopolisoituminen ja suuryhtiöden hallinta.* Helsinki, 1973.

Gruber, K. *Zwischen Befreiung und Freiheit*, Vienna, 1953.

Häikiö, M. *Suomi Englannin politiikassa.* Helsinki, lic. thesis, 1971.

Hakovirta, H. *Suomen turvallisuuspolitiikka.* Helsinki, 1971.

Halme, V. *Suomi ja maailmantalous.* Helsinki, 1962.

Harki, I. *Sotakorvausten aika.* Jyväskylä, 1971.

Heikkilä, T. *Paasikivi peräsimessä.* Helsinki, 1965.

Historiallinen aikakauskirja. Helsinki, 1958.

Hodgson, J. H. 'Finnish communism and electoral politics', *Problems of Communism* (Washington), Jan.–Feb. 1974.

Holsti, K. J. *Suomen ulkopolitiikka suuntaansa etsimässä vuosina* 1918–22. Helsinki, 1963.

Hyvämäki, L. *Vaaran vuodet.* Helsinki, 1957.

— 'Yhdysvallat ja YYA', *Kanava* (Helsinki), 7 (1974).

Hyvärinen, R. 'Puolueettomuuden valtioiden turvallisuus ongelma', *Tiede ja ase* (Helsinki), 23 (1965).

Irwin, J. *The Finns and the Lapps.* Newton Abbot, 1973.

Jakobson, M. *The diplomacy of the Winter War.* Cambridge, Mass., 1961.

— *Finnish neutrality.* London, 1968.

— *Kuumalla linjalla.* Porvoo–Helsinki, 1968. (This is the Finnish version of *Finnish neutrality.*)

Jalanti, H. *Suomi puristuksessa.* Helsinki, 1966.

Katsaus (Helsinki), 3 (1974).

Kennan, G. F. 'Europe's problems, Europe's choices', *Foreign Policy* (New York), 14 (1974).

Killinen, K. *Pääsihteerikilpa.* Helsinki, 1973.

Klemola, P. *Juuso Walden—viimeinen patruuna.* Helsinki, 1970.

Kleppe, P. *EFTA—Nordek—EEC.* Stockholm, 1970.

Klockare, S. *Yleislakosta kansanrintamaan.* Helsinki, 1971.

Komissarov, J. *Suomi löytää linjansa.* Helsinki, 1974.

Korhonen, K. 'Suomen puolueettomuuspolitiikka presidentti Kekkosen kaudella', in *Suomi toisen maailmansodan jälkeen,* ed. T. Perko. Turku, 1973.

— *Naapurit vastoin tahtoaan.* Helsinki, 1966.

— *Turvallisuuden pettäessä.* Helsinki, 1971.

Krymov, P. & Golovanov, K. 'Finland's foreign policy', *Int. Affairs* (Moscow), Oct. 1969.

Lafond, J-M. *Finlandisation.* Dijon, doct. thesis, 1974.

Lehmus, K. *Kolme kriisiä.* Helsinki, 1971.

Leino, O. *Kuka oli Yrjö Leino?* Helsinki, 1973.

Lundin, C. L. *Finland in the Second World War.* Bloomington, 1957.

Lyon, P. *Neutralism.* Leicester, 1963.

Lyytinen, E. *Finland in British politics in World War I and its aftermath.* Oxford, D.Phil. thesis, Sept. 1973.

Määttänen, S. *Tapaus Jakobson.* Helsinki, 1973.

Nevakivi, J. *Apu jota ei pyydetty.* Helsinki, 1972.

Nousiainen, J. *The Finnish political system.* Cambridge, Mass., 1971.

Ørvik, N. *Sicherheit auf finnische.* Stuttgart, 1972.

Pajunen, A. *Sarjatulta.* Helsinki, 1966.

Palmer, M. *The prospects for a European Security Conference.* London, 1971.

Parlamentaarisen puolustuskomitean mietintö. Helsinki, 1971.

Peitsi, P. (U. Kekkonen). *Tässä sitä ollaan.* Helsinki, 1944.

Pihkala, E. 'Suomen ulkomaankauppa vuosina 1945–72', in *Suomi toisen maailmansodan jälkeen.*

Pohlebkin, V. V. *Suomi vihollisena ja ystävänä.* Porvoo-Helsinki, 1969.

Puntila, L. A. 'Suomen kansainvälisen aseman kehitys toisen maailman sodan jälkeen', in *Suomen ulkopolitiikan kehityslinjat 1809–1966*, ed. I. Hakalehto. Porvoo-Helsinki, 1966.

Rintala, M. *Four Finns.* Berkeley, 1969.

Rossi R. 'Suomen EFTA-ongelma', *Kansantaloudellinen aikakauskirja* (Helsinki), 2 (1961).

Salonen, A. M. *Linjat.* Helsinki, 1972.

Seppinen, I. *Ulkopolitiikan puolustuspoliittiset tavoitteet.* Helsinki, 1974.

Shulman, M. D. *Stalin's foreign policy reappraised.* Cambridge, Mass., 1963.

Skog, E. *Sosialisti ja patriooti muistelee.* Porvoo-Helsinki, 1971.

Skyttä, K. *Presidentin muotokuva.* Helsinki, 1969, vols. i & ii.

Söderhjelm, J. O. *Kolme matkaa Moskovaan.* Tampere, 1970.

Thögersen, N. J. *De finske-sovjetiske relationer.* Åhus, lic. thesis, Dec. 1969.

Tiainen, H. *Kun puolue räjähti.* Helsinki, 1968.

Törnudd, K. *Soviet attitudes towards non-military regional cooperation.* Helsinki, Soc. Sc. Fennica, 1961.

— *Suomi ja Yhdistyneet Kansakunnat.* Helsinki, 1967.

Tuominen, A. *Myrskyn mentyä.* Helsinki, 1971.

Udgaard, N. M. 'Norway between East and West in World War II', *Cooperation and Conflict*, 2 (1973).

Upton, A. F. *Finland in crisis 1940–1.* London, 1964.

— *Kommunismi Suomessa.* Helsinki, 1970.

Väyrynen, P. *On muutoksen aika.* Porvoo-Helsinki, 1974.

Väyrynen, R. *Conflicts in Finnish-Soviet relations.* Tampere, Acta Universitatis Tamperensis, ser. A, vol. 47, 1972.

Virolainen, J. *Pääministerinä Suomessa.* Helsinki, 1969.

Vital, D. *The survival of small states.* London, 1971.

Wahlbäck, K. 'Finnish foreign policy: some comparative perspectives', *Cooperation and Conflict*, 4 (1969).

— *Mannerheimista Kekkoseen.* Porvoo-Helsinki, 1967.

Wolfe, T. W. *Soviet power and Europe 1945–70.* Baltimore, 1970.

Wuorinen, J. H. *A history of Finland.* New York, 1965.

INDEX